OUR TASK

HANS URS VON BALTHASAR

OUR TASK

A Report and a Plan

Translated by Dr. John Saward

A COMMUNIO BOOK

IGNATIUS PRESS   SAN FRANCISCO

Title of the German original:
Unser Auftrag: Bericht und Entwurf
© 1984 Johannes Verlag, Einsiedeln
With ecclesiastical approval

Cover by Roxanne Mei Lum

CONTENTS

CONTENTS

III. APPENDIX: THE EXERCISES
AS SEEN FROM HEAVEN

PREFACE

This book was first published because of the wish expressed by our Holy Father, John Paul II, in 1983 that a symposium on Adrienne von Speyr should be held in Rome. It took place in the fall of 1985. A symposium of that kind required the publication of Adrienne's entire works, and so in 1985, with the express permission of the Pope, the hitherto restricted posthumous works (*Nachlaßwerke*), which provide profound insights into her personal experiences, were made available to the general public. To many people these works will at first seem astonishing, perhaps even disconcerting. That is why the present book is needed. (It, too, was published, after some minor emendations asked for by Rome, with the permission of the Holy See.) It is intended to help the reader understand the ecclesial orientation of Adrienne's works, to see them as graces for a foundation within the Church. The reader should constantly keep in mind the interior connection between these three things. Many biographical matters, mentioned here only briefly and abruptly, will be explained more comprehensively by the detailed diaries. However, as I have often emphasized, whatever Adrienne experienced subjectively was meant to bear objective, theological, and spiritual fruit for the Church as a whole. This fruit is the criterion for judging the significance and genuineness of experience and becomes obvious to anyone who reads the writings already published. All the various aspects of her charism are directed concentrically at a deeper interpretation of revelation. That includes the developing community outlined here. Like all of Adrienne's work, it is intended to serve the whole Church.

I
REPORT

INTRODUCTION

This book has one chief aim: to prevent any attempt being made after my death to separate my work from that of Adrienne von Speyr. It will show that in no respect is this possible, as regards both theology and the developing community. At the same time, it is worth saying that no one should expect this to be a biography of Adrienne or my own autobiography. It is concerned solely with our common work. During Adrienne's lifetime, there were repeated warnings that the work entrusted to us might later be endangered. Adrienne once saw in the night "eight or ten black birds, facing each other in a circle". These turned into "demonic women", who did not want to pray. Some days later she saw Mary with the future community in her arms, and underneath her these same women, who, among the others, did not attract attention in a special way. She realized it would be "some of her own children who would gravely endanger the community, perhaps even try to break it up". Adrienne thereafter had to pray that "they would not do too much damage".[1]

---

[1] T [*Erde und Himmel: Ein Tagebuch* (Earth and heaven: A diary)] 922, 927. All the cited works of Adrienne von Speyr are published by Johannes Verlag, Einsiedeln. In the last volume of my *Theodramatik* [*Theo-Drama*] (as I indicate there) many of Adrienne's theological writings are cited. In this present work, it is the *Nachlaßbände* [Posthumous volumes] VII–X which are of chief importance. Volume VII contains *Das Geheimnis der Jugend* [The mystery of youth] and will be cited by the letter G and the appropriate page number. The entries in the three volumes of the diary (VIII–X) will be referred to by the letter T and

Another night she felt the walls closing in on her, to the point of crushing her to death. The message here was that the "walls" of the community should be built more solidly than at first envisioned.[2] "Betrayal will start from the very center of the Church."[3]

For Adrienne's biography, we have at our disposal her two descriptions of her life: one composed in written form (*Aus meinem Leben* [From my life]) and another where the story comes from the awareness she had of each stage of her life (*Geheimnis der Jugend* [Mystery of youth]). There are also the three volumes of diaries, *Erde und Himmel* [Earth and heaven], which continue the story from her conversion in 1940 to her death in 1967. These include some reminiscences of youth passed over in the other writings. Some biographical information has to be given in this report section in order to explain the back-

---

the number of the entry in question. *Das Geheimnis der Jugend* is based on the ability given to her confessor to "transfer Adrienne (back) to each of the various stages of her life, in order to run through her biography". This made it possible for her to recall much of what she had forgotten and provided far deeper insights into her interior life than a self-composed biography would have allowed. For example, in 1922 she burned a diary in which she had written down some prayers and short stories. In reply to my questioning, she reproduced a good deal of this diary. At each stage, she used the language she had spoken at the time—whether as a small child, as a high-school student, or as a medical student. This transferring of Adrienne back into her past (always in conversation with me) had a further effect, which for her was quite crucial: it gave me a presence in her earlier life. This pointed her each time toward a future that answered her questions (cf. G 186, 227, 274).

[2] T 1252.
[3] T 1729.

ground in our own two lives to the work we carried out together from 1940. The posthumous works are not yet generally available. Their circulation has been restricted up to now, so that Adrienne's objective message, which is so important for the Church, might first be heard and pondered.

There are some parts of Adrienne's complete theological works which, when taken out of context, may occasionally disconcert. When weighing up individual statements, readers of her works are implored not to lose sight of the complete whole that is her theology. The more one attends to the whole, the clearer the inner coherence of the parts becomes. However, such general exposition is not what this book is about; it would require a work many times larger.[4] Here I simply touch on the themes that are in some way or other common to her and to me.

I should also add that the extraordinary charisms of the foundress are not only meant to benefit the Church as a whole, as is evident, for example, in her scriptural commentaries, but also can and should have an even more specific effect on the daily life of the Community of St. John: for example, her understanding of the Communion of Saints in heaven and on earth, her view of the oneness of the "confessional attitude" (total openness) with love and obedience, the way she links deep contempla-

[4] Barbara Albrecht has made the first attempt at a survey in her two-volume work *Eine Theologie des Katholischen: Einführung in das Werk Adriennes von Speyr*, vol. 1: *Durchblick in Texten* (Einsiedeln: Johannes Verlag, 1972), vol. 2: *Darstellung* (1973) [A theology of the Catholic: Introduction to the work of Adrienne von Speyr, vol. 1: A look at some texts, vol. 2: Exposition]. See also the anthology of von Balthasar, *Kostet und seht* published by Johannes Verlag in 1988 after his death.

tion with down-to-earth action in one's secular profession, and so on.

There are very many different kinds of mission in the Church. Some are "alone with God, as Adam was alone with God at the beginning"[5]—for example, the mission of a St. Paul, a St. Augustine, a St. Ignatius.[6] "It would be quite wrong for such a person, who feels he has been sent, to start roaming the world looking for someone to complement him. Each of us has received from God what God gives him."[7] However, there are also "double missions", which complement each other like the "two halves of the moon". "The individuals concerned are first led along a complicated path, which was necessary to get them finally into the right kind of teamwork."[8] The model for this is the Crucified Lord bringing together Mary and John to form the virginal first cell of the Church (Adrienne often returns to this theme). Replicas of it include the collaboration of St. John of the Cross and St. Teresa, St. John

[5] T 1993.

[6] 1050–51.

[7] T 1993.

[8] Ibid. During A.'s student days she used to reflect on the obedience to be given if one has resolved (as she had done by studying medicine) to do the will of God. But what would happen if someone came to her "who really could say in the name of God, 'This or that is what the Bible means'?" She thought she would recognize the person concerned and his authority. "Something in you would respond, right away. . . . Now and then I think, 'Someone will suddenly come who really will know and hold the key. . . .' Now and then I feel like a sister waiting for her twin brother. I once made Mother furious on this account. I asked her whether I had perhaps assassinated my twin brother. I didn't mean, of course, murdered, but somehow caused his disappearance. . . . You know, we might have had a brother or sister who would be older than me" (*Nachlaßband* [= N] I/2, 255–56).

Eudes and Marie des Vallées,[9] and St. Francis de Sales and St. Jane Frances de Chantal. There can be double missions "where there is no external collaboration, and there are also doubtless cases where the decisive event takes place for the two parties concerned in the confessional".[10]

In our case, the plan was that we should collaborate intensively on a common external work. The long period of preparation (for Adrienne, from 1902 to 1940) was meant to make us ready for the complementary task. This involved two things. First, there was the great difference between our two paths. For Adrienne, there was the seemingly endless quest for Catholic truth, the medical profession, and the experience of marriage. For me, there was an education—first of all literary, then philosophical and theological—which was intended to give me a knowledge of the spiritual tradition of the Church, within which I could situate what was special and new about Adrienne's insights. Secondly, there was an affinity or association between us enabling what was different to become complementary.

This complementarity was once described as follows: "Again and again A. sees the mystery of the 'leaving behind' "—in other words, the leaving of the Son's divinity with the Father to make possible the abandonment on the Cross and thus the redemption. "To begin with, she does not understand what is shown her. . . . This is where the mission of H. U. comes in. For A. it is somehow a guiding principle when she speaks in the Spirit. She has to go into this 'speaking in the Spirit' until H. U. understands.

[9] T 1702.
[10] T 1993.

She has to explain until he sees clearly what is meant. And yet H. U. does not influence her. She just dissects, dismembers, the unified thing she sees. A. does not think that there is any great connection between these two facts —that I am theologically trained, and she is not. But it is true that contemporary theology is not (or not yet) in a position to understand what is shown. If someone reads A. and says, 'That's pure H. U.', sometimes they may be right. When A. sees yellow and H. U. sees blue, she may occasionally have to put herself into the position where he sees blue, so that she can lead him from there to where she sees yellow. There may be points in the speaking in the Spirit when H. U. outlines certain things. But this does not affect the final outcome, only the way to it. H. U. is her public. There is no other way." Nevertheless, "one of the things about the mission is that it takes place on an island to which there is no access.[11] But the whole relationship is most certainly for the Church and belongs to her. It is just that at the moment it does not have to be handed over."[12] Complementarity is only possible when the two halves are different. As for my path, Adrienne was told: "It is a different route, but the destination is the same."[13] Unlike some others, A.'s mission was not only one of experience, of the dark night and other christological states, but also quite expressly one

[11] This whole explanation was given when we tried to let a young Jesuit friend of ours sit in on one of A.'s dictations. A. broke off after a few words. It was no good. She could only dictate to her confessor. It was up to him to pass on the result to the Church.

[12] T 1994.

[13] T 325.

of interpretation. That is why a complementary mission was needed—to introduce and train her practically in the central christological mystery of the Son's obedience to the Father.[14]

This obedience was fundamental to everything. In the end it applied to both of us and was taken to its ultimate consequences. For me, the Society of Jesus was a "homeland", a gift that I loved above all things. Quite early on,[15] very quiet and gentle suggestions began to be made that the mission of St. Ignatius would perhaps be more important than remaining in the Society. A long period of uncertainty followed. This was intended to train me in detachment. In the end, I had to leave. The proofs for the correctness of the decision had meanwhile become overwhelmingly clear.[16] Taking responsibility for this was such a crushing burden for A. that she wished she could die, so that I could stay in the Society.[17] I guessed that was her wish and forbad her to make any such offer. I reminded her of the *maior gloria* motto. If God's greater glory "demands that I leave the Society of Jesus, then I am ready to leave. Nothing in the work of God must be diminished or altered on account of my refusal."[18] The

---

[14] We might never have had A.'s autobiography had she not written it in obedience to me. Cf. T 1507.

[15] T 430.

[16] T 1922.

[17] In Einsiedeln A. hears a voice: "Your fate is really too hard, because it includes the fate of H. U."

[18] T 1373. Cf. again at the death scene in Cassina. "*She*: I think if I go now you won't have to leave. *I*: We reached this point once before. But in no way do I want you to die so that I don't need to leave" (T 1598).

consequences of my decision were momentous. But they were slight in comparison with A.'s very different and yet complementary mission. In her series of death experiences, she was giving herself up more and more to the inner core of my mission. Finally, in March 1947, her continuing life will not only "be, more than ever before, a help for my mission",[19] but "A. feels that she is receiving her new life in order to bring my mission to completion." The christological significance of this decree was explained to her in detail: the relationship of the Incarnate Son to the Father.[20] These apparently extravagant ideas will be fully clarified in what follows. To bring out the interwovenness of the two missions, it is best if they are mentioned in advance.

We must describe, first, the two quite separate roads leading to the final collaboration, secondly, that collaboration itself in two parts: the theological and spiritual work, and then the foundation of the community, for which, as was said at the beginning, this book specially came to be written. The report section comes first only because it helps to shed light on the spirit of the community sketched below. That is the chief subject of interest, but without further explanation it would seem rather colorless.

---

[19] T 1748
[20] T 1751.

A. THE WAYS OF ACCESS

1. Adrienne's Path to Her Conversion

Adrienne fought long and hard to come into this world.[1] From childhood she was rejected by her mother and bullied by her older sister.[2] As a small child she had a vision of her guardian angel, who showed her that the horizons of truth for her mother and for her were different, that we should not be defensive about the way we pray and do penance. She described in writing the encounter she had on Christmas Eve 1908, when she was six, with St. Ignatius Loyola: above all he "radiated poverty".[3] As an old woman, she remained absolutely convinced of the reality of this meeting.[4] The angel taught the little girl to make the letters IL with cardboard tiles (this was the man who sent the angel to her), and then the letters IJ: "The first one is the same man as before, and the second one is his friend. His name is John. But who he is", adds the little girl, "I do not know."[5] It is Ignatius who will later send the disciple John to explain his Gospel to her.[6]

[1] *Aus meinem Leben* [From my life] (1968) (= AL), 41.

[2] T 1468. Very late on, she succeeded in winning over her mother (T 2216).

[3] T 2347.

[4] AL 25f.; and for important details following the apparition: G 89–90. In her early youth there were several other mystical phenomena. She once saw the Crucified Lord hanging on a wooden pole with a cross-beam that had been erected on a building site (T 24). On another occasion (in 1908) she was snatched up into heaven and set down in a different place (T 1637).

[5] G 24.

[6] T 1100.

Ignatius will tell her that "he only got to know and love
John really well in heaven. In fact, were he to come back
to earth now and set up his community again, it would
probably be much more Johannine."[7] This mysterious
information did not as yet make much sense to the little
girl, but it had the effect of making the Protestant religion she had been given (with its strong anti-Catholic
bias) seem inadequate and sent her off on a decades-long
quest for the things it lacked. At school she once wrote
"of her own free will" an essay on "Prejudices". This is
how she describes its content: "They don't like talking
to us about other religions because they want us to keep
our blinders on. The blinders are all the things they leave
out of the [New] Testament." She showed the essay to
her father, who commented, "A lot of this is very Catholic."[8] Later she gave a talk on the *restrictio mentalis* of the
Jesuits. This outraged the other girls, but, according to

[7] T 1136; cf. 1301. A. says of Ignatius that "the transformation he
has undergone in heaven is remarkable. In some way on earth he demanded too much of himself; he, as it were, pressed the nib too hard.
In heaven everything has loosened up. . . . That is why he has come
close to John" (T 1301). On the attitude of the two saints, see T 2324.

[8] G 21. In the hospital for a chronic appendicitis operation, she declared to a clergyman who visited her: "I am not a Protestant. You
needn't bother yourself with me" (AL 78). This provoked a storm of
indignation from her mother. "You'll see, this child is going to become
a Catholic. . . . She certainly does enough stupid things to need to go
to confession" (AL 80). In 1914 the pastor who often accompanied
A. home after religious instruction, and with whom she used to speak
about the Gospel, said to her now and then: "That's Catholic. Where
did you get it from? Who put that in your head?" (AL 102). Her friend
Madeleine said to her once, quite casually and to A.'s great astonishment: "It's best if you know all this before you become a nun. Then
you'll have a bit of the course behind you" (AL 125). When she was

one classmate, "she vigorously defended herself and convinced us all."[9] With a friend she founded a society for converting their classmates to God.[10] This same friend told her that she, Adrienne, would become a nun.[11] At the age of fifteen she had a "pictorial" vision of Mary, which was of decisive importance for the future. "The whole thing was like a picture, and yet the Mother of God was alive, in heaven, and the angels were changing places. . . . I saw it in a kind of wordless prayer. I was amazed, full of wonder. I'd never seen anything so beautiful. . . . I wasn't frightened, just filled with a new, strong, and very gentle joy . . . , although at the time I don't think I had a clue I was going to have to become a Catholic."[12] At the same time she received a wound, which never closed, in the area of her heart. When she saw me for the first time in 1940, she knew that I was the one for whom she had been waiting and for whose sake she had received the wound.[13] When she was still small, the angel told her: "From now on you'll always be sick for a short time before Easter." Why? "He said,

---

a student, it "suddenly [became] clear to [her]. Protestantism was the opposite of a promise. It was a kind of step backward" (AL 308).

[9] T 184; AL 34.
[10] AL 122.
[11] AL 124. Cf. 315 and T 1644.
[12] G 25.
[13] G 45, T 1637, 1645, 1680, 1729–30. Later, when the book about the prime numbers within the ecclesial number 153 was being dictated, the following was pointed out: "A. received the wound on November 1, 1917. 19 = Vianney (the patron of confession), 17 = Francis (the fullness of the Gifts of the Holy Spirit), the eleventh month = Ignatius (= All Saints' Day)" (T 1672).

'Because of Good Friday.' And the illnesses are not very nice. . . . You feel sick, you have a headache or such a bad stomach-ache that you can't read. Or you're so tired that you can't do anything. You just feel awful."[14] After the vision of Mary and the physical wound, she is clearly aware of a "mystery" in her.[15]

From her youth, in her quest for truth, she read a great deal,[16] but before her conversion she came across very little that was Catholic. She felt very strongly that two things in particular were missing in the religion she had been taught: "In all these stories (the ones they tell you in Sunday school) there is no mother; the children were like orphans." A returned missionary explained to her that on

---

[14] G 21–22.

[15] G 47. "Now I know", says the twelve-year-old child, "*we* will never get married" (G 76).

[16] On Adrienne's reading: from her childhood she read "much" (G 21, AL 71, 82). At high school her friend Charles-Henri Barbier chose what she should read in her "voracious appetite for reading" (AL 85). In Leysin she read Dostoyevsky (AL 164), "the whole of Victor Hugo", and also, though with little pleasure, the funeral orations of Bossuet (G 31). On our second meeting, we talked about Péguy and Claudel. In the diaries there are incidental references to philosophy (she went to some of Haeberlin's lectures), Plato (in conversation with Heinrich Barth), Goethe (in school: "We have read Goethe all year. It is not complete", G 61), Hölderlin, Keller, Hofmannsthal, the latter's letters to C. J. Burckhardt, Nietzsche, Storm, Reinhold Schneider, Rilke's letters, and Annette Kolb, with whom we were both friendly. This is by no means a complete list. In addition, she was familiar with French literature and read lots of French novels, especially women writers, because they were interested in human destinies. She occasionally read things to help me with my work, but very little that was really theological (St. Thérèse of Lisieux, a little Newman, a very little St. Teresa of Avila). Around 1934 she read Karl Adam's *Wesen des Katholizismus* [*The Spirit of Catholicism*] (G 303).

the missions there were the wives of the missionaries and women teachers. "Quite obviously [says young A.] the man hadn't understood at all."[17] The answer for what was lacking was only given when she had her vision of Mary and, after her conversion, came to enjoy an incredibly intimate contact with the Mother of the Lord. The second thing, which she sought desperately, with a kind of rage, was real confession. A Catholic patient with whom she sat up in Leysin made his confession to a priest. "[She was] beside herself", she said, "I'd like to go to confession! And then die! Mustn't tell Mother. Because I'd like to see God!"[18] At every stage of her life there is the same passion: "Always having to think about this confession!"[19] "Couldn't I confess to you, just to have a try?"[20] As a medical student she revealed her deepest desires. She would like to be allowed to obey, but that would require a community, not just a "*tête à tête* with God", and that in turn would involve confession, someone who can reconcile you with God. "Let me confess, just once!"[21] True, she can pray, but "I lack obedience. I give consolation and advice when I (myself) am uncertain." On one occasion at school, when she had misunderstood one of her fellow pupils, a Catholic, she tried to ask everyone for forgiveness. She also went to the different sects where sinners publicly confess their guilt, but she always came away disappointed. Later, as an intern, when she was cel-

[17] AL 46–47.
[18] G 32.
[19] G 36.
[20] G 42, NB I/2, 254.
[21] G 130.

ebrating Christmas on her own: "I lit the candles on the
little Christmas tree, sat down in front of it, and tried to
confess. But I couldn't do it sitting, so I knelt on the floor.
The moment I tried to tell God everything, I couldn't remember anything. . . ."[22] It continued like this through
the years: "Oh, if only I had confessed!"[23] She decided,
out of compassion, to marry Professor Emil Dürr with
his two boys, but something did not seem right: "Is it
because I haven't confessed that things aren't right?"[24]
Then in her medical practice: People tell you so much,
she says to herself, so surely you should be straightened
out yourself. "Do you hear confessions?"[25] Her husband
had come close to the Church and had visited churches
with her in Corsica. She spoke to him "about confession
and about the Church, the hierarchy, and about the possibility of there being several Churches of Christ alongside
one another, even though there should only be one."[26]
After Emil's death: "I'm like a spare train on a side track.

[22] G 188.

[23] G 201.

[24] G 227. Adrienne was maneuvered into this marriage by a clique of
Basel friends and acquaintances. Some remarks of the time: "I really
think not. Absolutely not. Somehow there is a mystery of the soul and
a mystery of the body." "Occasionally I think: After all, every woman
must have a purpose . . . because an old maid is nothing." "But I feel
such terrible pity for him." "I feel so frightfully sorry for him." So
in the end she says Yes (G 222–30). Again during the first marriage:
"What ought I to confess, if I could confess here and now?" But first
she has to become a Catholic. "If you are a Catholic, can you live and
pray out of fullness? I believe this fullness exists, but I don't know
where it is" (250). "Can't I confess now? Why this delaying tactic?"
(G 264).

[25] G 266.

[26] G 288.

And I'd like to confess. I'd like to be one of those people who are allowed to be in the true Church of the Lord."[27] Conversion will finally fulfill her longing for confession, in other words, for the official power of having sins forgiven. From this will come her dictated book on confession and a host of insights into confession in her other books and diaries. But that is not all. The experience will also help her understand the deep connection, of which she already had an intuition, between confession and ecclesial obedience, and it will imprint on her what for her is a central concept—the "confessional attitude", the permanent and fundamental openness of the whole soul to God and to the appropriate confessor or superior. She will assess the perfection of the saints in terms of the perfection of their confessional attitude.[28] She even speaks of Mary's confessional attitude and demands that this be the attitude of the members of the future community.

Her development has a third characteristic. From her youngest days she wanted to dedicate her life to God and her fellow men—but in a very profound way, which involved the idea of substitution. As a small child, when accompanying her father, who was an eye specialist, on one of his visits to the hospital, she asked whether she could be blind for a time, so that a blind child might see. At the age of eight she asked a young diabetic, who was nibbling candy and shortly afterward died: "Would it be easier for you not to eat chocolate if you knew that I wasn't eating any either?"[29] She was certain from a very

[27] G 311.
[28] Especially in *Allerheiligenbuch* N I/1, I/2.
[29] AL 23–24.

early age that she wanted to become a doctor, like her
father. She fulfilled this ambition with iron determination, despite all the objections of her family, and paid her
own way through her medical studies by doing tutoring.
Only one temptation troubled her from time to time—
to study theology, so she could learn more about God.[30]
"All her medical studies and practice were seen as an act
of obedience to God."[31] There was one other important
factor: her passionate love of music. She had begun playing the piano at about the age of ten, but she "constantly
had to break off from it because of back pain."[32] At the
Töchterschule in Basel she took lessons with the famous
conductor Münch and had to practice three hours a day.[33]
During the hard years when she had been rejected by her
family and was feeling very lonely, "making music occupied an ever-larger part of my life. I more or less reveled
in it and hoped through music to come to God . . . so
that I could offer my life to him without reserve."[34] In
the end she realized she "could not do both—medicine
and music. . . . And so I decided to sacrifice music for
the sake of my future patients. I thought it would enable
me to get closer to them, that it would be better if I ap-
proached them with a renunciation behind me."[35] Her
uncle, director of the Waldau psychiatric clinic in Berne,
who was himself a fine pianist, asked her why she did not
play any more: "I didn't say how very hard the sacrifice

[30] G 247.
[31] T 1665.
[32] G 121–22.
[33] AL 206.
[34] AL 219.
[35] AL 223.

had been for me, nor, on the other hand, how I knew for certain that medicine, as I saw it, from the outset called for sacrifice. The significance of the sacrifice might not be immediately obvious, and yet for that very reason, just because it was a sacrifice, it could be demanded and used by God according to his will."[36]

We can see in these interconnected motives a foreshadowing of what Adrienne will later consciously and deliberately uphold: the unity of wholehearted adherence to God and an equally wholehearted commitment to men in one's secular profession. She lived out in advance the future community's pattern of life. If we add to this her longing for ecclesial obedience and her truly radical poverty[37] in the years of her illness (in Leysin) and study, then we have an exact model for the uniting of life in the evangelical counsels with life in a secular profession. And her insight into the possibility of substitution shows that, in her understanding of life, there was already an outline of the Catholic idea of the Communion of Saints, which was to play such a central role in her work, both theoretically and existentially. One final thing becomes clear from her prehistory. She was from the beginning meant to belong to God totally, and yet the choice between marriage and virginity could not yet be a reality for her.[38] The

[36] AL 236.

[37] G 267: "Eventually . . . I experienced in my innermost being what it means to be a beggar."

[38] G 222: "There is not a third thing." She was already saying this before her marriage to Emil Dürr. It will remain a fundamental principle in her Catholic life: T 1935, 1952, 2338. Becoming a Protestant deaconess did not appeal to her: cf. the chapter on Saint-Loup in AL 187–95. True, this would have involved the renunciation of marriage,

experience of marriage, which she could not avoid, was
of benefit not only to her professional work but also to
her profound thinking about the "theology of the sexes"

"but there was never talk of a vow of celibacy. . . . As long as one
thing does not completely exclude the other, there is bound to be
compromise." Cf. G 204. To understand her decision to get married,
we have to appreciate the impasse in which Adrienne as a Protestant
found herself at the time. "I firmly believed I was meant to be celibate,
but I did not see the form it could take. It seemed to me that a commitment was necessary. I saw that, like marriage, it was a commitment to
God, but how?" "What is virginity [*Jungfräulichkeit*]? Something that
is eternally young [*Etwas ewig Junges*]? Something that doesn't exist in
Protestantism?" (G 120). Celibacy seemed to her, even then, "to be
the only possible way" for a theologian (even a Protestant one), "but
how?" (AL 247–48). Before her marriage to Emil: "Deep down I don't
have the feeling that I am doing what God wants. And yet I should
be doing God's will even less if I were *not* getting married now. . . . I
have such a strong feeling of being sold" (G 233). "Perhaps there are
martyrs who somehow get hopelessly enmeshed, trapped" (G 235).
She learned to love Emil Dürr greatly for his nobility of soul and for his
love and was deeply depressed by his early death, but she sees the heart
of her marriage in the following way: ". . . that we are created for what
God wills, not for what *I* want. That is what I mean by *purity*. Somehow
the bodily aspect fits in with that." Married life would then only be
"impure if one had no pure intentions" (G 241). She entered into her
second marriage with Werner Kaegi despite the "greatest misgivings"
(G 296), again as if taken unawares (G 298). Compassion once more
played the key role: "I had this quite impersonal feeling: he needs a
wife. And he wants to do good, but he is so insecure in life. It didn't
occur to me that he needed *me* as his wife" (G 297). A little later:
"He needed a wife. After all, if he loves me, why shouldn't he get me?
And then there are the children [from Emil's first marriage] . . ." (G
299). Although there was genuine affection, the relationship was not
an altogether easy one. The marriage was not consummated, and so
A. was later able to take a vow of virginity. Without the hospitality
of Werner Kaegi, my work with A., and later my residence on the
Münsterplatz, would never have been possible (cf. T 1646).

(grounded in the Christ/Church relationship) and, in general, to her insights into the positive value of bodiliness in the religion of the Incarnation. However, as the diaries describe, she was given back her virginity. The central power which got her through the seemingly endless years of searching was the constantly expressed feeling: "God is different."[39]

To complete the picture of Adrienne's development, we need to say a little more about her character and the situation in which she lived, though unfortunately many vivid and informative episodes will have to be omitted. From the beginning she was incredibly exposed and yet amazingly protected. She was protected by an innocence that always marked her out. The angel taught her to forgive and forget all the injustice surrounding her. She bore no grudges. Evil did not tempt her, though there was much that made her sad, and later in her time as a Protestant she lost sight of the meaning of life and came close to suicide.[40] Somehow, from the beginning, she lived beyond the reach of any kind of concupiscence. Her rich uncle, who was himself a doctor, refused to pay for her medical studies because he wanted to shield her from its crudities. (In fact, they made no impression on her.)[41]

[39] AL 154, 101, 145, 163, 184, 227.

[40] Cf. the scene by the Rhine after her mother had thrown her out of the apartment (AL 207ff.), and after the death of her first husband (AL 292f.). In the first case she held herself back; in the second she was stopped by her friend Franz Merke.

[41] Despite the very crude and summary explanation of sexual intercourse which had been given in Leysin (AL 183), even in medical school (where two good friends protected her from anything indecent) she did not really know much about the male organs (G 292f. n.), even

She studied the subject so that she could serve God and man, and serving man meant serving him in body as well as soul. From high school onward people flocked round her: "I have loads of boyfriends. I could marry a different one every week if I wanted to!"[42] She was friendly with Walter Eichrodt, Heinrich Barth, Adolf Portmann, Franz Merke, but instinctively drew away were anything erotic to develop.[43] In Berne, when she was eighteen, she was the object of an almost incredible attempt at seduction by a very well-known doctor, who, with his wife's permission, wanted to have total possession of Adrienne and tried in every way to ensnare her. In the end nothing happened to her.[44]

She was marked by humor and enterprise. She was like the boy in the fairy tale who sets off to experience fear. At her mother's instigation she had to leave high school but secretly studied Greek at night by the light of a candle, so she could keep up with the others. In Leysin she learned Russian. After her transfer to the high school in Basel, she quickly learned German and at the same time took a crash course in English to catch up with the rest of the class.[45] As I have said, she paid for her medical studies by

---

though "for a time she frequently had to fit men with catheters, which each time involved taking hold of the male organ. This . . . made not the slightest impression on her" (T 1699). There are "a good many things one does not understand at all. About intercourse with men" (G 170).

[42] G 137.

[43] G 199.

[44] G 50f., 104f. On A.'s innocence, T 1705.

[45] AL 131f., 173, 176, 202, 206.

tutoring. Then there is her courageous readiness to stand up for justice. When a teacher struck a boy in the face with a ruler, she rushed forward, turned the teacher to face the class, and shouted: "Do you want to see a coward? Here's one!"[46] On one occasion in the lecture theater an intern gave an injection to a patient which promptly killed him. The intern falsely blamed it on the nurse and was defended by the professor. Adrienne got her fellow students to boycott the professor's lectures for so long that he had to move to another university.[47] It was precisely this courage, maintained in the face of the most extreme physical pain,[48] which enabled her after her conversion to take on, for decade after decade, every kind of spiritual and bodily suffering, especially participation in the agony of Christ in Gethsemane and on the Cross. Indeed, when later she realized its significance for the reconciliation of the world, she constantly asked for it.

Even before her conversion, there was a kind of premonition of what was awaiting her. "Do you know what? Now and then I think that I'm going to have a hard life."[49] Sometimes she took "the good Lord by the hand, so to speak, so that he could do with me what has to be done. . . . I suspect there are certain sorrows which the good Lord gives a person, a certain kind of horror at sin, a certain kind of inability to endure. . . . That is what is so unsatisfactory about medicine: you can't take on to your-

---

[46] AL 68. In the same place she describes the scene when, at the age of twelve, she slapped the face of a schoolteacher because of the latter's unfair treatment of an innocent, not very able girl; cf. N I/2, 251.

[47] AL 299, 302f., G 157–61.

[48] AL 270ff., G 124ff.

[49] G 114.

self what's happening to the person in pain."[50] "There are some things one can imagine. But I cannot imagine having real anxiety. . . . I once told the good Lord that if ever he wanted something of me, simply as a present, he could have it. But then, when I thought about it, I had to laugh: I'm a cheeky soul. . . . He may just suddenly take it seriously. And then how would he cope with this Adrienne person? You see, if it was going to be a genuine present, I should have to bear it properly. I should need composure."[51] And during her illness in Leysin: "Is it not so that a person can have a totally darkened spirit before death?"[52] In fact, that is how it was when she herself died. As she had asked it should be, her death was a hard one.

During her youth Adrienne did not give up the works of penance familiar to her since her instruction by the angel. She never took analgesic medication for headaches and other severe pains. She did penances just as they occurred to her: "stones in the shoes", which she could not remove in college, "otherwise everyone would ask how they came to be there"; beating herself with an instrument. "I think you have to offer up the pain."[53] This was a rehearsal for what came later, when the penances she did for the sins of the world, which she had been shown, could hardly be kept within reasonable bounds.

During her first marriage she had three miscarriages, each of which was an intense strain.[54] They occurred at

[50] G 195-96.
[51] G 175.
[52] G 38.
[53] G 112.
[54] T 1650.

the time I was making my decision to "become a priest and religious. It was the answer to the dawning awareness of my mission."[55] Moreover, as I have said, since her vision of the Mother of God, A. bore a wound in her heart. The fifteen-year-old said to me: "You're the one I got this wound from." In the vision she saw me kneeling by the side of Mary. "You do realize, don't you, that I got your wound, and that the good Lord put you in it."[56]

2. My Path to 1940

There is far less to report. I was born in 1905 into a straightforwardly Catholic family. Only my maternal grandfather was a Protestant. He had been an army officer and was very much on the edge of the family's life; from time to time we would pay him nervous visits in his smoky, weapon-filled room. I grew up with a faith that was equally straightforward, untroubled by doubt. I can still remember the silent and very moving early Masses on my own in the choir of the Franciscan church in Lucerne and the ten-o'clock Mass in the Jesuit church, which I thought was stunningly beautiful. In my early years, I read a great deal, but nothing religious. My mother walked daily to Mass down the steep path leading from our house; without doubt it is to her prayers and her early and painful death that I owe my late and very sudden vocation to follow the way of St. Ignatius. (The call came during an Ignatian retreat for lay people.)

[55] T 1662.
[56] G 26. Cf. T 492 (instead of "girl of seventeen", read "girl of fifteen").

The years before I went to high school were taken up mainly with music. From the time of my first, overwhelming musical impressions (Schubert's Mass in E-flat major when I was about five, Tchaikovsky's *Pathétique* when I was about eight), I spent endless hours on the piano; then at Engelberg College I had the opportunity of taking part in orchestral Masses and operas. When some friends and I transferred to Feldkirch for the last two and a half years of high school, we found the music department there so noisy that we lost the inclination to play. During my semesters at the university, an abundance of concerts, operas, and orchestral Masses made up for the poverty and near-starvation conditions of postwar Vienna. I had the privilege of lodging with Rudolf Allers—physician, philosopher, theologian, translator of St. Anselm and St. Thomas. In the evening he and I would play a complete Mahler symphony in keyboard arrangement for four hands. Then came the retreat already mentioned. When I joined the Jesuits after completing my doctorate, music was automatically at an end.

I find it hard to describe my spiritual life up to this time. Untroubled faith, devotion to our Lady, but certainly not enough prayer. Sermons and religious instruction almost always bored me. Hans Eibl's lectures on Plotinus in Vienna, which I attended when I was studying German literature, were probably the roundabout route by which I came to an interest in theology. Allers, who had started off as a disciple of Alfred Adler but had found true *communio* in the Catholic Church, also played a part in interesting me in genuine theology. I had taken up the study of philology out of love for German literature; I also did

THE WAYS OF ACCESS

some philosophy, Sanskrit, and Indo-European linguistics. It never occurred to me to consider what I would do with all this knowledge in later life. Only much later, when the lightning flash of vocation was already several years behind me, did I understand. When I had completed my philosophical studies at Pullach (chaperoned at a distance by Erich Przywara) and my four years of theology in Lyons (inspired by Henri de Lubac) in the company of my fellow students Daniélou, Varillon, Bouillard, and many others, I came to see how very helpful my knowledge of Goethe, Hölderlin, Nietzsche, Hofmannsthal, and above all of the Fathers, to whom de Lubac pointed me, would be for the working out of my theology. The chief postulate of my work *Herrlichkeit* [*The Glory of the Lord*] was the capacity to see a "form" in its interconnected wholeness. I wanted to apply Goethe's way of seeing to the phenomenon of Jesus and the convergence of New Testament theologies. The Fathers had a similar way of seeing, which retains its validity despite the whole modern tendency to analyze everything.

When I look back on the subject of my dissertation and the book that developed out of it, *Apokalypse der deutschen Seele* [Apocalypse of the German soul], I see that its fundamental impulse was the desire to reveal (*apokalyptein* means, of course, "to reveal") the ultimate religious attitude, often hidden, of the great figures of modern German literature. I wanted to let them, so to speak, "make their confession". The work was of insufficient maturity —most of the chapters ought to be rewritten—and yet some of it may still be valid. Przywara's influence on my first attempts at philosophy is obvious, even though I

later moved away from his tendency to extreme negative
theology and tried to reinterpret him in line with my own
views.[1] Clearly my translation of part of St.
Augustine's *Enarrationes* on the Psalms (1936) came about under his
influence, and from that came the more comprehensive
Augustine anthology, *Das Antlitz der Kirche* [The face of
the Church] of 1942 (my hope was to provide something
more readable to replace Przywara's brilliant *Augustinus:
Die Gestalt als Gefüge* [Augustine: The figure as struc-
ture] [1934]). Impressed by his dialectical interpretation
of St. Thomas' real distinction,[2] I was able to find my
way to my later friend Gustav Siewerth (who admittedly
engaged in fierce polemics with Przywara) and still later
to Ferdinand Ulrich, to whose views I owe so much in
the concluding part of *Herrlichkeit* III/1 [English translation, *The Glory of the Lord* IV], and indeed in the *Theodramatik* [*Theo-drama*] as well. These men, especially the
latter, helped me see the intellectual history of the West in
its totality and to appreciate the Christian and theological
presuppositions of the more recent history of philosophy.
To de Lubac and his rediscovery of the doctrine of the
fourfold sense of Scripture (as found in Origen and then

---

[1] My first attempt was in 1933: "Die Metaphysik Erich Przywaras"
in *Schweizerische Rundschau* 33:489–99. The "reinterpretation" is in
my introduction to Leo Zimny's bibliography: *Erich Przywara: sein
Schrifttum* [Erich Przywara: his writings] (Einsiedeln: Johannes Verlag,
1939). Later I brought out a three-volume edition of those of Przywara's
works which, in my opinion, have a permanent validity. At the same
time, of course, I had to include the somewhat extravagant second part
of *Analogia Entis* (Erich Przywara, *Schriften* I–III [Einsiedeln: Johannes
Verlag, 1962]).

[2] Cf., for example, E. Przywara, *Ringen der Gegenwart* (Augsburg,
1929), vol. II, 924ff.

in general Christian tradition) I owe my abiding convic-
tion that modern exegesis only retains its usefulness, its
truly indispensable usefulness, when it does not forget the
divine fullness of the Word in revelation. Without these
pioneers, I would have been incapable of understanding
and communicating, with any reasonable degree of competence, the dictated works of Adrienne von Speyr in the
exactness of their insights and the almost immeasurable
variety of their theological opinions.

In view of what is to follow, I should also briefly mention here the authors who particularly attracted me during my theological studies and those of their ideas which
fascinated me. Above all, there were four Greeks (my interest in St. Augustine was very much in second place).
First, there was St. Irenaeus, the anti-Gnostic theologian
of the enfleshing of the Word. In contrast to all the Christian mystical theology influenced by Neo-Platonism, bodiliness was to play a key role in Adrienne's theory of mysticism.[3]

Secondly, there was the mighty Origen. De Lubac had
introduced us (Daniélou and me) to him. I wrote a condensed essay in French about him[4] and later published an
anthology of about a thousand texts from his writings.[5]

[3] Cf. her work *Subjektive Mystik* [Subjective mysticism] (1980), her
Theologie der Geschlechter [Theology of the sexes] (vol. XII of the posthumous works), and many things in her diaries.
[4] "Le Mystérion d'Origène", RSR 26:514–62 and 27:38–64, later
as a book, *Parole et mystère chez Origène* [Word and mystery in Origen]
(Paris: Cerf, 1957).
[5] *Origenes: Geist und Feuer: Ein Aufbau aus seinen Werken* (Salzburg,
1938, 2d ed. 1952; English translation: *Origen: Spirit and Fire* [Washing-
ton, 1984]).

The two points in his immense work which fascinated me
can be stated simply. First is his eschatology (in contrast
to Augustine's) with its tendency to universal redemption.[6] It was clear to me that an unqualified doctrine of
apokatastasis was irreconcilable with the Church's theology. On the other hand, Augustine's certainty about a
(densely) populated hell seemed to me to be unscriptural.
But how could one find a middle way, or rather a third
solution over and beyond the conflicting alternatives? At
the time I did not know. It was Adrienne's Holy Saturday experiences which were to open up a quite startling
way of rethinking the whole question. Later I looked for
approaches in the history of theology into which I could
incorporate her teaching. I tried to explore this possibility in several writings, first in *Das Herz der Welt* [English
translation, *The Heart of the World*] (written in 1943, first
published in 1945), then in *Die Gottesfrage des heutigen
Menschen* [The God question of modern man] (1956), in
"Eschatology" (1957),[7] and in most detail in *Theologie
der drei Tage* (1969).[8] It cannot be by chance that, in her
encounters with the saints, Adrienne will feel "most at

[6] In his penetrating study of the commentary on Jeremiah 20:7 ("O
Lord, thou hast deceived me!"), Cardinal de Lubac has shown that Ori-
gen does not simplistically support a theology of universal redemption
(Einsiedeln: Johannes Verlag, 1984).

[7] In *Fragen der Theologie heute*, ed. Feiner/Trütsch/Böckle (Einsiedeln: Benziger, 1960), 403–21. Included in *Verbum Caro*. Skizzen
zur Theologie I (Einsiedeln: Johannes Verlag, 1960), 276–300; English translation: "Some Points of Eschatology", *The Word Made Flesh*.
Explorations in Theology I (San Francisco: Ignatius Press, 1989), 255–
77.

[8] Reprinted from *Mysterium Salutis* III (1969), 133–326; English
translation: *Mysterium Paschale* (Edinburgh, 1990).

THE WAYS OF ACCESS

home with the Church Fathers" and "especially close"
to Origen.[9] She meets him "with special love and reverence".[10] The other theme in this master's work which fascinated me was his repeatedly expressed idea that Christ
came upon his Bride, the Church, when she was a pros-
titute (she had fallen from heaven to earth), and that by
his redemptive work he was able to change her back into
a virgin. I later pursued the theme through the whole
of patristic literature in a larger study and assembled the
texts under the title—taken from St. Ambrose—of *Casta
Meretrix*.[11] I had no idea, when I was doing this work,
that one day what I was describing would be fulfilled in
an unfathomable way in the married Adrienne.[12] In this
way, she would truly be *personam ecclesiæ gerens*, as the Fathers say.[13]

The third person who greatly preoccupied me during
my studies, and about whom I wrote a book,[14] was St.
Gregory of Nyssa. He fascinated me for quite different
reasons. The first was his well-known theory of the secondary character of human sexual reproduction, a theory
which has its roots in Origen.[15] Adrienne would later of-

[9] T 2086.
[10] T 1626.
[11] In *Sponsa Verbi*. Skizzen zur Theologie II (Einsiedeln: Johannes
Verlag, 1960), 203–305; English translation, *Spouse of the Word*. Explorations in Theology II (San Francisco: Ignatius Press, 1991), 193–288.
[12] T 1645.
[13] T 1644–65.
[14] *Présence et pensée: Essai sur la philosophie religieuse de Grégoire de Nysse*
(Paris: Beauchesne, 1942) [Presence and thought: Essay on the religious
philosophy of Gregory of Nyssa]. (English translation in preparation.)
[15] As Georg Bürke proved later in "Des Origenes Lehre vom Urstand
des Menschen", ZKT 72 (1950): 1–39. Cf. also my *Christlicher Stand*

ten make allusions that are reminiscent of these speculations.[16] The second theme was the coincidence of movement and rest in God and in the eternal life of the saints, repeatedly described in texts which I have expounded with particular joy and care.[17] Adrienne quite independently took up this theme in her trinitarian doctrine and elsewhere.[18] In *Endspiel*, I based my own reflections on both Adrienne and texts from the Fathers.[19]

I had studied, written about, and translated the last Church Father, St. Maximus the Confessor, before ever I met Adrienne. In Maximus all the streams of the Greek patristic tradition flow together in synthesis. At the same time, with real originality, there is much from within that tradition that he takes to a higher level.[20] But the course

(Einsiedeln: Johannes Verlag, 1975), 76–81; English translation: *The Christian State of Life* (San Francisco: Ignatius Press, 1983), 95–103.

[16] T 1427 and *Theologie der Geschlechter* (N XII), passim.

[17] Both in the French book (footnote 14) and in the anthology of texts from the commentary on the Song of Songs, *Der versiegelte Quell* [The sealed spring] (Salzburg: O. Muller, 1939, new edition published by Johannes Verlag, Einsiedeln, 1954, and revised version based on the critical edition published in the meantime, Johannes Verlag, 1984).

[18] For example, in *Die Welt des Gebetes* (Einsiedeln: Johannes Verlag, 1951), p. 67; English translation, *The World of Prayer* (San Francisco: Ignatius Press, 1985), and frequently in other works as well. Cf. G 245: "The ocean may seem endless. But the ocean is an image of eternal life. . . . It is ever different and yet ever lovely and ever full."

[19] *Theodramatik* IV, 57ff., 80ff.

[20] *Kosmische Liturgie: Höhe und Krise des griechischen Weltbilds bei Maximus Confessor* [Cosmic liturgy: The summit and crisis of the Greek picture of the world in Maximus the Confessor] (Freiburg: Herder, 1941). Considerable changes were made for the second edition (Einsiedeln: Johannes Verlag, 1961), and several translations, together with the study of the "Die gnostischen Centurien des Maximus Confessor"

of this saint's life impressed me even more than his teaching. Once again, like Athanasius, one man was able to defend orthodox Christology against a whole empire. A Byzantine joins forces with Pope St. Martin I in Rome and finally suffers martyrdom for the true faith. This is the summit of that unity of doctrine and life which marks the whole patristic age; speculation and mysticism of the greatest subtlety are wedded to a soberly and consciously grasped martyrdom. In St. Maximus we can see in the *Catholica* what Kierkegaard found within the individual.

That key word *Catholica* brings me to the last figure to become important before (and for the sake of) my meeting with Adrienne: the experience that is Paul Claudel. A student friend in Lyons introduced me to the *Soulier de Satin* [The satin slipper] and the *Cinq Grandes Odes* [The five great odes]. I was fascinated by his view of Catholicity, and by 1939 I had done German versions of both works. I later revised and added to the translations in many different ways. I was well aware that the dramatic action of *The Satin Slipper* was problematic, but two things outweighed my reservations: the writer's boldness in giving planetary dimensions to the love of a man and a woman, and his determination, in the spirit of Dante's *Divine Comedy*,[21] to describe the painful transfiguration

(Herder, *Theol. Studien* 61 [1941]) were added. (English translation in preparation.)

[21] See the magnificent "Hymn on the Sixth Centenary of Dante's Death". Certain of the themes of *The Satin Slipper* can be discerned in T 1427. For example: "It doesn't work without humiliation. Even the chaste husband feels it when he has to take this course in order to possess his wife."

of Eros into pure Agape. It happens first to the woman.
Taught and purged by the angel, she sacrifices herself
and is transformed into a guiding star. Then she drags
the reluctant man toward the final blessed humiliations.
It seemed to me that what eventually happened when I
met Adrienne (who in any case was already far removed
from Eros) was a kind of transposition of this drama into
a very different sphere. Throughout my patristic studies,
what I longed and looked for, with the strong encour-
agement of Henri de Lubac (cf. his major work *Catholicism*), was a catholicity that excluded nothing. And then
in Claudel, though in complete form only in Adrienne's
theology, I found it. She had been looking for the same
catholicity and found it in the Catholic Creed and in the
bountiful exposition of that Creed which came to her
from heaven.

Adrienne emphasized the absolute necessity of catholicity as vigorously as I have done from the beginning.[22] I
have tried constantly to bear witness to it—most recently
in my little book *Katholisch* [English translation, *In the
Fullness of Faith*] (1975).

In this section I have only touched on those of my
books written before I met Adrienne. Two things become clear. First of all, through my literary, philosophical, and theological education a means was provided for
assimilating the fullness of her theological insights and
giving them appropriate expression. (We are not talk-

---

[22] Cf. only T 798, 895, 1640 ("The gift of faith, which enabled her
to see the faith as an undivided unity"), 2116 ("All the parts are taken
up in the whole, and there they receive their conclusive meaning").
There can be no question of anything like a "canon within the canon".

ing here about a mechanical process. Adrienne's involvement in the verbalizing of what she had seen spiritually
demanded cooperation on her part. On the other hand, it
also required a kind of Catholic view and Catholic vocab-
ulary on mine.) Thus there were times when I was able
to work out what or who it was she was seeing but could
not properly describe. One night she saw the prayer of
"a St. Gregory", but she did not know his name. However, once she had described his prayer, it became clear
to me beyond doubt that it could only be St. Gregory
Nazianzen.

B. OUR COMMON
THEOLOGICAL WORK

1. Adrienne's Early View of the Foundation

Adrienne was received into the Catholic Church on All Saints' Day 1940. Soon afterward she said to me: "God is always looking for people who at the decisive moment will not be afraid."[1] The first thing she was told that she could expect was suffering (in which a God-given anxiety would play a key role). She would be asked relentlessly whether she was ready, in all seriousness, to give up everything.[2] But just before the first real experience of the Passion in Holy Week 1941, as she said in a letter (March 30, 1941), Mary appeared to her. "She advised me to devote myself to young women. So many vocations can be found there in embryo which should be helped to develop."[3] From now on she begins to consider "the possibility of a new community". "She makes notes about everything she doesn't like or that seems to be missing from existing orders and congregations. She knows a number of educated young women who certainly don't belong in a regular monastery but who ought to leave the world for a period of recollection and spiritual formation and then return to the world at full strength."[4]

It was now that for the first time she got to know the

[1] T 9.
[2] T 36.
[3] T 40.
[4] T 95 (June 9, 1941).

47

supernatural world in all its dimensions—from heaven to
hell. Numerous promises were made, and equally numerous miraculous healings took place at her hands. The theological mission in the stricter sense would begin (with
the dictations on St. John's Gospel in May 1944) only
when she had been sufficiently initiated into the mysteries of the Passion and the new life that flows from it.
But chronologically, the community she was called to
found came first. In July 1941 she presented the basic
idea to me. She saw different circles: a "core group" of
the best educated, a "second circle of the less educated,
auxiliaries, and finally a third circle of people with a loose
association with the community. The best personnel can
be put into the most important positions in public life."
"A long period of preparation and formation is necessary."[5] It is important to point out here that neither she
nor I had the slightest inkling that at this very time there
were various other similar experiments taking place. It
was only in 1947 that they were given status in canon
law by Pope Pius XII (in *Provida Mater*, followed by other
documents).[6] The result of this lack of knowledge was
that at first, when students for whom I had conducted the
Exercises felt themselves called to the life of the evangelical counsels, I tried to send them to the various orders,
especially the Society of Jesus. As late as 1948 I published
a little book with the wrongheaded title *Der Laie und der
Ordensstand* [The layman and the religious state] (instead

[5] T 107.

[6] The Church documents relating to secular institutes have been
collected by Jean Beyer with a foreword by H. U. von Balthasar (Einsiedeln: Johannes Verlag, 1963).

of . . . *der Rätestand* [The state of the evangelical counsels]).[7]

Adrienne's preoccupation with the community she had been asked to found (she now usually called it "the Child") became more and more intensive. "My prime time belongs to the Child, in the sense that a lot of things are now being quietly examined, reflected on, and somehow prayed over. Statutes and vows are the main thing at present." She began to make notes about them.[8] A few days later she sees Mary in front of her "(not a vision, but really there, *en chair et en os* [in flesh and bone]), with the Child on her arm". She sees houses, large and small, "full of life and work". A. is prompted to new reflections and notes, which she proposes to show me.[9] I went to visit her with another priest. She showed me her notes: "Nothing but notes, but in their precision they testified to a clear overall view of the whole. Much of it was inadequately expressed because of her lack of knowledge of ecclesiastical regulations . . . or because the matter was already dealt with in the Code in a different way."[10] In November Adrienne wanted "to give a talk to the women students'

---

[7] *Der Laie und der Ordensstand* (Einsiedeln: Johannes Verlag, 1948; 2d ed., Freiburg: Herder, 1949; new ed.: *Gottbereites Leben* Freiburg: Johannes Verlag, 1993).

[8] T 136–37. "The Child is at the happy stage where each new day brings a little progress" (T 138). A person well known in Switzerland is in the same hotel. This sets off inner conflict with her until A. realizes that she has to settle her "for a time outside the Child", in a state of "mortification", which may eventually lead her to the new community: T 143. Further visions of Mary with the "Child" in her arms (T 222, 355, 673, 937, 949, 1885).

[9] T 145.

[10] T 147.

circle and invite the girls afterward to her home."[11] In the Spring of 1942 she had a conversation with a troublesome Jesuit, who told her that the founders of orders had always been saints. I had to disabuse her of this idea, which really upset her (because she never wanted to be taken for a saint), and added: "Of course, we shan't be founding grand orders as St. Ignatius or St. Francis de Sales did. It will be more modest." To this she replied: "It will become something great. It will spread out. . . ."[12] However, much that she saw on her visits to the hospital made her "anxious about the progress of her future daughters".[13] When she was suffering the anxiety laid upon her, she was still able to pray "in joy" for the coming community.[14] On one occasion, when she was really depressed about the community, she opened the Bible at random and read this: "Do not be afraid. Henceforth you will be fishers of men."[15] She prayed constantly for the "Child" and learned a great deal about it. She also prayed for my "inadequacy", so that I would be able to cooperate properly.[16] And, more than anything else, she

[11] T 231.

[12] T 261.

[13] T 268.

[14] T 273. She then explains more precisely: "Our daughters should not, must not, be like the nun who told her that the reason she was exerting herself was that she did not want the last place in heaven. 'Our people' must never think of themselves in their work." Although one may for a time pray for one's own salvation, "the time will still come, at least for us, when we are there just for others . . . total service and self-oblation" (T 274).

[15] T 287.

[16] T 309. "We simply *must*. God is waiting for our assent." A. "sees clearly how far mine is from being perfect" (T 312).

wanted to "teach" the "Child" "the spirit of penance".[17]
She once saw the Lord from afar: "This distance signifies that there is a path she has to walk: she must 'build'
the 'Child' and through the 'Child' go to the Lord."[18]
As for her spiritual life, she said that "the 'Child' and
the general task always stood at the center of the visions.
There are more and more things to learn. . . ." It was
also important to communicate it to me. She maintained
that I would "profit from it almost as much as she, even
though I saw nothing of her visions".[19]

   In the following months, A. suffered much for priests.[20]
The idea came up, albeit indistinctly, that we should have
a task in relation to the clergy.[21] In early January 1943,
when returning home from her office, A. heard "a voice
seeming to demand harshly that now is the time finally
to get the 'Child' going." But the means shown was, for
the time being, not heightened action, but intensified suffering: "loneliness on the edge of hell", God's love experienced only as "an iron law, as hard as diamond", in
fact "the possibility of leading an utterly meaningless life,
just to obey God",[22] the experience of final damnation.[23]
But she urged me to start giving the Exercises soon to the
first women students.[24] The next few months overflowed

[17] T 384.
[18] T 411. Cf. T 509. Mary tells her that "the way is still long. *Ap-
prendre, souffrir, progresser* [to learn, to suffer, to make progress]."
[19] T 450.
[20] T 353, 375, 390, 461, 464, 471, 494f., 513, 592.
[21] T 478.
[22] T 521.
[23] T 550, 564.
[24] T 590.

with terrifying visions. A. went through all the horrors
of the war. She had to experience the psychological state
of the tortured and starving, of people burned to death,
and of the torturers. She saw scenes of the Passion and
practiced excessive penance; overwhelmed by what she
had seen, A. sometimes forgot the limits I had imposed
on her. Throughout this time she continued to meet and
introduce herself to women students. Meanwhile, apparitions of "St. Ignatius and many lay people in the Church,
including and especially women. A. says it is quite wrong
to claim he has nothing to do with women."[25] On one
occasion, she was reading the biography of Mary Ward,
which "left her with a terrible impression: the wrecking
of a great mission because of the disinterest of authority. For some days she saw the fate of the 'Child' in this
light."[26] For a whole night A. lived in different monasteries and was given the kind of rich insight into each order that she would have had "if she had lived in each of
the monasteries for ten years". "She saw exercises that
do not take sin seriously but from the outset steer toward a happy ending. And there are exercises that build
everything round a single point, so that eventually God
becomes a function of Dear Little Me and my religious
needs." Then "she saw the importance for the 'Child' of
a long and thorough preparation. We shall have to resist
the temptation to make do with some exercises and a few
bits of advice in place of the apostolate, a kind of quick
laundering instead of real action."[27] In October she had a

[25] T 725.
[26] T 743.
[27] T 821.

vision of a Mary "who had rejected the offer of God. She would have been a devout Jewess. She would have lived a life without fear. . . . But there was an emptiness in this picture which became more and more unbearable." Then A. herself was "faced with the choice: life without anxiety and without the 'Child', or life with the burden. For a moment the burden is shown her, as it were, from the outside. . . . In these circumstances, it is not hard for her to say Yes. But no sooner has she uttered her assent than a cloud of anxiety, shame, and despair descends upon her. In the break beforehand she saw that the 'Child' really is on his way and that we have got to make an immediate start."[28] Soon after this she spent a whole night thinking about "monasteries and the world" and "sketched out a number of things".[29] Later, in the hospital, there is rapture: "She is standing by a very pregnant woman, who radiates, almost physically, a great human warmth. The woman asks A. for her medical and human assistance at the birth. A. agrees, and at that moment she realizes it is Mary. The Mother disappears, but the child she was carrying was *the* Child. Mary immediately reappears as the Virgin Queen of Heaven and now promises her help with the birth of the 'Child'."[30] In November A. was in deep despair. "She no longer believes in the 'Child', even though it is supposed to be founded in a few days, on December 8." It was also at this time that she had the vision of the black birds mentioned at the beginning of this book. On December 8, in the chapel of the residence

[28] T 857.
[29] T 869.
[30] T 874. Cf. T 880, the vision of the "Child".

hall, with A. very cold, we met with four women students for a Marian celebration. "Afterward we gathered round A. and discussed the community. Each person described how she saw it and what the first thing to do should be. . . . We decided to meet occasionally, meanwhile to unite in saying the *Suscipe*, and to spend a little time each day in meditation."[31] After this there were all kinds of instructions about how careful we ought to be about admitting members.[32] We were also to have a clear knowledge about the writings of false or erroneous women mystics.[33]

After Easter 1944 Adrienne was shown how important prayer would be in the new community. "In addition to obligatory prayer, space should be provided for personal prayer. This is even more important for the women than for the men." To her horror she was shown what she would look like if she no longer prayed. "She saw herself wrapped up in activism and externals: the shell, the dead skin of her earlier life. Christians who stop praying are hard to save."[34]

In May 1944 the dictations on St. John's Gospel began

---

[31] T 920, 944.

[32] T 980, 1009, 1047, 1055, 1091. Genuine obedience in the state of the evangelical counsels depends on everyone, especially superiors, having "the right stature for it" (T 1022). Some of the candidates I had guided into the Jesuit novitiate came out (T 1234). "We were told that *we* were the ones who hadn't been listening properly. . . . For the sake of the 'Child', we had to learn to be attentive to the fortunes of the candidates. . . . The new *parents* really ought to bear responsibility for the birth" (ibid.).

[33] T 993–94, 1153.

[34] T 1088.

and continued throughout the year. At the same time we
were urged to get on with the proper launching of the
community.[35] In the spring of 1945 for the first time A.
saw alongside Mary and the "Child" "some priests connected with the work" that was to begin. It also became
seriously clear that I might eventually be forced to leave
the Jesuits.[36] I should then have to look after these priests
as well. In June we looked for a house for the community in Basel. At night A. had a vision of a certain parish
priest, who was friendly with us, and of an empty floor.
On the strength of that, I told the priest something of
our plans and asked him whether he knew of a house
for us. "He leads me to a house, *Wettsteinallee* 6, which
can be rented."[37] On August 5, in Estavayer, we had the
Exercises which were the real foundation of the community. (The visions of the Apocalypse began during them.
The pregnant woman in chapter 12 is the one who before
had asked A. to give her assistance at the birth.) On our
return, the priest offered us the "complete fitting out" of
the community house from an inheritance he had been
left: "furniture, kitchen equipment, and a cellar with coal
and firewood". Other friends went out of their way to
show kindness, and so by the end of September the house
was completely fitted out and by the beginning of October could be occupied by the first three members.[38] The
house was blessed after a celebration of Holy Mass. "We

[35] T 1200.
[36] T 1293.
[37] T 1326.
[38] T 1357–58.

go from room to room and pray together on our knees in each place."[39]

The later fortunes of the community need not be described here. In this chapter what matters is simply to show how much the idea and planning came from A. She was constantly persuading me of the urgency of this task and also of my responsibility for the whole thing, which in the end was the cause of the hardest sacrifice that could have been asked of me: to leave the Society of Jesus.[40]

It was only after I had left that it became increasingly evident that a men's branch should be founded in addition to the one for women.[41] Something will be said about this later. And since it was now less possible to guide priests wanting to live the evangelical counsels into the novitiate of the Society, the plan emerged for a branch of what soon after would be called a "secular institute" (*institutum sæculare*) for diocesan priests.[42]

2. The Dictated Works and How They Were Composed

We have seen that, in a way she could not explain, I was already present in the decades of A.'s searching. I for my

[39] T 1368.

[40] T 1293.

[41] T 1529.

[42] Cf. T 1520: "First priests, then they can bring in the seminarians." For lay people: T 1508. Quite early (August 6, 1941), A. described in a letter a vision of the coming community: alongside a large number of women she sees a small number of men (T 145). Later the proportions even out.

part sensed and foresaw nothing of our future collaboration. From her childhood, Adrienne felt herself to be connected "for better or worse" with the Jesuits—without having any clear idea of what Jesuits were.[1] My theological formation took place in a totally objective way. It was to prove to be a useful instrument for the work we did together.

Initially, we just had a few catechism sessions on the Catholic faith. I was amazed by the way A. immediately grasped everything she was told, as if it were something long expected.[2] The decisive thing at the very beginning was the fact that I "gave her back" the Our Father. This came about as follows. When Emil was close to death, she went to the hospital chapel to pray fervently that he might live. "I promised God everything, if only he would leave me Emil. I kept on praying the Our Father."[3] When her husband died, she felt she could no longer say the petition "Thy will be done." "I don't want to lie to the good Lord." In the churches in Rome that she visited she felt "excluded, so to speak, because I can no longer pray. . . . Sometimes I feel I am dying of longing." Why, then, was she no longer praying? "If I did, I'd risk returning to the situation where I do what *I* want."[4] A Protestant clergyman advised her to avoid the Our Father and say other prayers instead. But then she felt a kind of emptiness, "the absence of God, in fact, almost the nonexistence of

---

[1] T 93.

[2] On A.'s state of health during her convert instruction: N I/2, 258–59.

[3] G 291.

[4] G 300.

God".[5] One of the first instructions I gave her was about
simple, unselfconscious praying of the Our Father, which
at a stroke gave her back all her prayer.[6]

Something strange happened at her (conditional) baptism, which she experienced as "something very real".
("She says that she believes she was already validly bap-
tized, and yet something new was added at her Catholic baptism").[7] As she recited the Tridentine profession
of faith, she stumbled as she came to the words about
the Catholic Church "*extra quam est nulla salus* [outside
of which there is no salvation]" and left them out. Her
husband, who was there, said he heard the words quite
distinctly but as if spoken by a strange voice.[8] As soon
as A.'s extraordinary experiences began, my work con-
sisted chiefly in fitting them into the tradition of the
Church and convincing this down-to-earth doctor that
"they involved nothing 'abnormal' ".[9] For a long time it
was difficult for her as a doctor to bring her two lives together.[10] I tried to lead her into "an ever-closer interweaving of the two existences",[11] which in time succeeded.[12]
She was forbidden to engage in any kind of psychological reflection on her "states". She would say that "what
was happening to her was not real mysticism. . . . These
things had nothing to do with her, with poor old, bad

[5] G 300–301.
[6] T 47. "From this point on I prayed like a lunatic" (T 2274).
[7] T 103.
[8] T 235.
[9] T 26.
[10] T 41, 51, 58.
[11] T 67.
[12] T 95.

old Adrienne."[13] For reading, I recommended the letters of St. Ignatius and St. Thérèse of Lisieux. Ignatius' letters, she said, were "the most glorious thing she had ever read".[14] She later translated St. Thérèse's *Story of a Soul*, which was published by our publishing house, though it was eventually made obsolete by the critical edition of the *Autobiographical Writings*. A year later, in a letter, she asked me to teach her "a little theology".[15] "I ought to acquire a thorough knowledge of Catholicism, so I can pass it on to others."[16] I never gave A. any proper instruction in theology. She heard my homilies[17] and the instructions I gave to the community. Over the years she would help correct the proofs of my books,[18] which after 1941 were greatly influenced by her wealth of ideas.[19]

Once she had grasped what the *communio sanctorum* meant for Catholics, the bearing of one another's burdens, she began to practice so many penances of the severest kind that I was constantly obliged to restrain them.[20]

[13] T 77. A. fought against the idea of being a mystic ("Protestantism has given her a great horror of mysticism"). She had to be taught that even "unworthy people" in the Church may receive apparitions. She replied that "the apparitions she had were not visions at all, just simple reality. . . . It truly was actuality, ordinary reality, and by comparison the other kind (earthly reality) was almost unreal" (T 195). Under no circumstances did she want to be confused with a saint (T 261).

[14] T 27.
[15] T VIII, 43.
[16] T 179.
[17] T 1442.
[18] T 1073.
[19] See below.
[20] T 59.

She always obeyed—when she remembered the ban. The trouble was that from time to time God gave her the grace to see the needs of the Church, the terrible poverty of those years, and the horrors of the war with such immediacy that she simply forgot the limits imposed upon her and just threw herself into penance. "I'm afraid I've done something stupid again", she would say afterward.[21] She had also devised for herself a lengthy program of prayer that could not be carried out without much toil and trouble on her part. It was not difficult to set her free from the quantitative approach to prayer.[22]

So far so good: just the regular problems of "spiritual direction". The question that exercises the reader of Adrienne's books is the extent of my own involvement in them. This problem came up only with the start of the dictations proper in May 1944. Two points must be underlined. First, she had complete freedom of initiative in receiving what was given her and in translating it into a human language that I, who had to take down the shorthand, could understand. Secondly, I did to some degree help her to prepare for giving the dictations. Adrienne was adamant that they should be given in an "ecclesially precise" way. My role was mainly to set her free from any self-reflection and to let the whole process be carried out in an atmosphere of trusting obedience to the Church (represented by her confessor).[23] From my references to

[21] T 66, 132, 236 and passim.

[22] T 8, 222, 228.

[23] T 1700. From the very beginning A. did not "feel the slightest need to speak with anyone except [me]" (T VIII, 42). Later: "It is an essential part of the mission that it is carried out on an island to which

St. Ignatius and in the spirit of his *Suscipe*, A. developed, first practically and later theoretically, her rigorous theory of "subjective mysticism": one has to surrender oneself completely, without introspection, so that what has been shown by God will be received undiluted.[24]

At first, the dictating was hard for A. I submitted the shorthand version of the commentary on St. John's Prologue (which is difficult by any reckoning) for her approval. She gave it a critical reading, made some corrections, and eventually reworded it.[25] Very soon, though, her dictating became so fluent, her sentences so well formed, that she herself abandoned the idea of checking everything, and I was able to transcribe what she said without difficulty. Occasionally, she would circle around the idea she was trying to articulate, using various expressions, until she found the right one, which would be the only one that needed to be printed. At other times, the exact word would occur to her in her mother tongue. I would sometimes leave the French word in the text or put it in brackets after the German. Her statements would sometimes be made so pithily that I could not grasp the exact meaning, and she had to break off (which was an an-

---

there is no access. But the whole relationship is meant for the Church and belongs to her" (T 1994).

[24] See especially her book *Subjektive Mystik* [Subjective mysticism] (1980), but also the numerous criticisms, made throughout all her works, of those mystics, male and female (including some famous ones), who seemed to her to lack this attitude of total availability. There is much on this in *Das Allerheiligenbuch* [The book of all saints] (N I/1) and the "exercises of readiness" in the same book (I/2, 129-38).

[25] T 1166.

noying distraction, requiring her to find her way back to her original composure). However, the explanation given in a few sentences was so enlightening that it was worth the disturbance. Now and again, unfinished sentences had to be completed for printing, words were transposed, and so on, but nothing essential had to be changed.

What form did the inspiration take? A. said it was "very variable". It could be given "partly in words, partly in gestures and intimations", or simply by the showing of "great connections".[26] "When she dictates, A. translates what she has seen—the *species impressa*, as it were." What was shown could then remain, so to speak, in store "in order to be brought out again later at the time of dictation. At that moment everything is once more in place, as fresh as ever, even though months have passed. The ideas are absolutely clear; they do not need to be looked for. The only matter that requires occasional consideration is the language to be used to express the ideas. Then A. asks me not to write for a moment but just to listen. She explains the thing to me, perhaps with some images and analogies, and then I write down a continuous paragraph, as faithful as possible to these illustrations."[27] This is another reason why it may be possible in a number of dictations to detect my "style".[28] But the most important reason why

[26] T 1121. Cf. 1942, 1944, 1948, 2015, 2025, 2128–29. On the difference in inspiration between the dictations on St. Paul and those on St. John, see T 1893.

[27] T 1225. On the precision with which the dictations are given, see T 1700.

[28] It was clear to her that what she had seen in heaven had to be transposed into concepts and images that I could understand (T 205). But her mission on communication (to the Church): "She maintained

A.'s dictated works—all of them without exception—do not in any way depend on "suggestions" from me is the originality of her theology (compared with mine up to this point) and, despite the vast number and diversity of themes, its astonishing coherence. She sometimes corrected me in my opinions.[29] She was well aware of the limits of theological language,[30] but the precision of her statements distinguishes her clearly from so many mystics who think that one can only stammer about God. There may have been an interplay here between her own intelligence and love of clarity and the concepts she learned from me when she was being instructed.[31]

It was a different story with Adrienne's countless experiences of abandonment. She was not permitted to see any meaning in them. As her confessor, I had to explain that, despite everything—yes, really!—what was meaningless to her had vitally important meaning for the Church and for the world.[32]

---

that I would profit from it almost as much as she did, even though I saw nothing of her visions" (T 450).

[29] For example, T 435: "No, you cannot say that"; (T 448): "A. says it just is not true at all . . ."; cf. (T 518) and passim.

[30] For example, with regard to a correct statement about *simul justus et peccator* (T 156). "She often complains that she cannot express what she knows. . . . She came to me with a wonderful picture which she wanted to show me. But I only saw the frame. . . . She would like at least to describe the picture, when I cannot see it" (T 242).

[31] T 1975.

[32] Very often. For the frightening experiences with M.'s child, see T 190. ("I tried as best I could to show her the meaning. . . .")

3. Adrienne's Themes

Any attempt to summarize Adrienne's highly original theology faces the problem of deciding which thread in the thick fabric to extract first. Her themes cover all the tracts of theology—from trinitarian doctrine and Christology to ecclesiology, from protology to eschatology. We could start with the things she missed most acutely and sought most persistently during her Protestant youth: confession (together with the ecclesial office authorized to give absolution) and the Blessed Mother (and in Mary the creature's perfect attitude to God). The two apparently isolated themes point to one and the same center. Behind confession as sacrament lies the permanent "confessional attitude": standing naked before God and before the Church with her Christ-endowed authority. For Adrienne, this showing of oneself is both the condition and the content of obedience, which flows not from coercion but from love. That is how St. Ignatius always saw it. Now the obedience of love is revealed only in its full and final form in the Christology of St. John's Gospel, where the Son's whole life of obedience to the Father appears as nothing other than the expression of his perfect love for the Father, for his will and the mission he has given him. From this point one path leads back to the doctrine of the Trinity. The incarnate obedience of the Son is based on his eternal attitude of love and readiness toward the Father, and the Father shows reverence for the divine freedom of the Son, while the two forms of eternal love are united in the Holy Spirit. Adrienne's trinitarian doctrine, which always has a christological starting point, has opened up completely new aspects of this mystery. The other path leads to the final consequences of the world-redeeming obedience of Christ. Here Adrienne unlocks a hitherto scarcely developed part of the theology of redemption. On Good Friday the Son's love renounces all sensible contact with the Father, so that he can experience in himself the sinner's distance from God. (No one can be more abandoned by the Father than the Son, because no one knows him and depends on him as much as the Son.) But then, after Good Friday, comes the final, the most paradoxical and most mysterious stage of this loving obedience: the descent into hell. In Adrienne's new experience and interpretation of hell, this means descent into that reality of sin which the Cross has separated from man and humanity, the thing God has eternally and finally cast out of the world, the thing in which God never, ever, can be. The Son has to go through this in order to return to the Father in the ultimate obedience of death. He has to encounter this deepest cesspool of estrangement from God, the product of misused human freedom. Here we see, to use the language of logic, that the complete contradiction of divine truth has been infiltrated by the complete obedience of the sent Son and thus by the divine truth of God himself. The implications of Adrienne's Holy Saturday and other "hellish" experiences—for theology, mysticism, and ordinary Christian life—are incalculable and will have to be studied slowly and carefully.[1] In so doing, we must not forget that, for Adrienne, despite all attempts at clarification, this expe-

---

[1] The descriptions of these experiences are found chiefly in N III and IV.

rience remained an absolute mystery, resisting resolution
into the formulas of any "dialectic".

Of course, there can be no journey from these christological themes to the ecclesiological ones unless there is
a road to connect them. For Adrienne, the vital bridge
is Mariology. Her first book, which she planned on her
own, was about the Mother of the Lord.[2] Later, in the
diaries and in a recent publication,[3] there followed subtle
meditations on our Lady's place in God's saving work.
Mary is seen in close connection with John. From the
Cross the Lord makes the two of them together the virginal first cell of the living community of the Church.[4] As
we shall show later, the community that Adrienne and I
were to found was meant to be guided into this primordial
cell of the Church, the unity of Mary and John.[5] Moreover, as the first chapter of his Gospel shows (1:42) and
the whole of its conclusion (chapters 20 and 21, which
Adrienne expounded at great length), John is linked most
closely with the office-mission of Peter. John forms the
central link—albeit one that steps back and disappears—
between Mary, the innermost core of the *Ecclesia immacu-
lata* (Eph 5:27), and the office of Peter, which represents
the unity of the Church: another reason for establishing
the future community on this foundation.

---

[2] *Magd des Herrn*, written in 1946, first published in 1948 (2d ed.,
1969); English translation: *Handmaid of the Lord* (San Francisco: Ignatius Press, 1985).

[3] *Maria in der Erlösung* [Mary in the redemption] (1979).

[4] T 1011, 1116, and passim.

[5] In the church at Einsiedeln, A. once saw Mary and John, and then
spelled out the name for her daughters: *Filles de Saint Jean et de Marie*,
[Daughters of St. John and of Mary] (T 1667).

When one looks at Adrienne's ecclesial theology in its rich diversity, the first thing that stands out is that she has the typical realism of a medical doctor (like St. Hildegard). The sacramental aspect of the Church is not at all neglected—as can be seen from the book on confession, the commentary on Holy Mass, her little book on the seven words from the Cross, and many entries in the diaries. However, four aspects are particularly significant for her.

Although she had the experience of marriage, physical virginity was later restored to her by the Lord.[6] In the light of the mystery of Christ and his Church (the Bridegroom and the Bride, Eph 5) and of the Mary-John (mother-son) relationship, Adrienne looks at, and explains, the relationship of the sexes in Christian marriage. She looks with a realism that goes into specific details, but, like St. Paul, she is dominated by a vision of the higher mystery. This must never be forgotten when studying her *Theologie der Geschlechter* [Theology of the sexes].[7] It is from the preeminent fruitfulness of virginity that the bodily fruitfulness of man and woman gets its justification and sacramental hallowing. The order of creation is incorporated into the christological and ecclesial order of redemption. This helps us understand why in every area of theology and spirituality Adrienne placed such emphasis on bodiliness and embodiment. In contrast to many others, the religion of Christ is one of permanent incarnation (in the resurrection of the flesh). Adrienne was suspicious of, indeed really hated, any kind of one-sided spiritualization

[6] T 1644ff.
[7] N XII.

(smuggled in through foreign influences). Here again she is like the great woman doctor Hildegard.

The second ecclesiological theme is based on the key christological concept of mission: "As the Father has sent me, even so I send you" (Jn 20:21). The Mystical Body of Christ does not rest on abstract principles but on concrete persons who have missions, or on missions which are personal. Every Christian has some kind of task, a mission, but for the Church there are certain fundamental missions—Adrienne calls them "differentiated" missions—which represent essential aspects of the Church, "pillars" (cf. Rev 3:12) which visibly or invisibly bear the weight of the Church. They are all different, but mutually complementary, within the all-encompassing holiness of the Church. In a rather strange work of Adrienne's entitled *Das Fischernetz* [The fisherman's net],[8] the number 153 (the number of fish in Peter's untearable net) is the embodiment of this all-encompassing holiness. Each of the indivisible prime numbers contained within the fullness represents one of the fundamental missions of the Church; when it is added to the other prime numbers, which have an influence on its mission, it makes up the total number of the Church. This is not the place to illustrate the subtle mathematics of this amazing work, but it is typical of Adrienne, in the sense that for her the obedience of earth can and should correspond exactly and adequately to the plans of heaven. The more adequately a saint corresponds to his mission, the more selflessly, unselfconsciously, transparently he prays and lives, the

[8] N II.

more perfect he is, and the easier it is for God through him to carry out his will "on earth as it is in heaven". The two of us were certainly taken into consideration in this work, because we were shown only saints we knew, saints whose way of life could teach us something. It also became clear that this heavenly mathematics infinitely surpassed our powers of comprehension. The final calculations—the numbers, their relations, intervals, and so on —were shown us just in passing and not given further interpretation.[9] The important thing for what now follows

---

[9] Different aspects of number mysticism can be found in the diaries. This number mysticism began at the same time as the visions and dictations of the Apocalypse, which are also Adrienne's exclusive property: T 1335 (the first seven prime numbers, which together add up to 153); T 1342 (the significance of 153); 1404 (addition and multiplication of numbers), 1416, 1481, 1503 (during a dictation A. said: "From the feast of St. Ignatius to the end of the year there are 153 days"), 1605 (possible faults in the saints), 1692, 1711 ("God wants above all to show that these key positions exist. . . . It was, however, clear to H. U. that there was much in the Church which had to be different, but previously he saw only an empty space. Now he sees how such spaces are filled"), 1785 (when I was summoned to see the Father General on April 22 in Rome, St. Ignatius said: "22 = twice 11"), 1808 (on false numbers, i.e., persons who pass themselves off as indivisible missions —there is a great deal about this in *Das Fischernetz* [The fisherman's net]), 1845, 1918, 2022 (on the different forms of the saints' obedience, which are divided out of the unity, only then to be gathered back into the unity. "One hundred fifty-three is the sum total in which all the individual forms of obedience are integrated, and the individual forms come from it through a breaking down, a differentiation, which is only Christianly possible if the differentiation—in its differentiatedness—is made up to the total number. There would, therefore, be no point in studying one saint by himself, describing him in isolation, showing how he is worthy of imitation, if one did not show him at the same time as a single door into the totality of the Lord. . . . All

is the idea of corresponding to one's mission. This leads us
back to Christ, who in his loving obedience forever perfectly fulfills the will of the Father, and to Mary-Church,
who through all the difficulties of her mission, including
the things she does not understand, corresponds exactly
to her mission. Her loving readiness (which is the same
as what St. Ignatius called *indiferencia*) becomes the basic model for all holiness in the Church. There can be
no doubt that in this way Adrienne attained a purity of
soul that we can compare to an undamaged photographic
plate: everything, heavenly and earthly, could be reproduced on it. It was a purity that came through the suffering given her as a share in the Passion, through her thirst
for vicarious penance for all that is wrong in Church and
world, through her almost incomprehensible familiarity
with the Mother of the Lord. On her countless "jour-
neys" she was transported to places in the world where
trouble of some kind was taking place. She would then
be transported into the soul of, say, someone who was
finding it hard to make his confession, so that she could
give him inner help. In this way, she was able to support the dying, people being tortured and burned alive in
concentration camps, men on battlefields and in prison,
in fact suffering of every kind. This transparency is the
presupposition of what follows.

---

the saints must be transparent to the Lord. One should be able to see
him, illuminated by the saints, though at the same time they should
have their own light, their form, their relief, so that not everything is
dissolved into the form of the Lord. . . . There is always, and at the
same time, both universalization and individualization"), 2335.

The third ecclesiological theme becomes clear in Adrienne's *Allerheiligenbuch* [Book of all saints].[10] In this book she was shown the prayer of a host of Christians, the saintly and the not so saintly, within the *communio sanctorum*. She then described this prayer in a short summary. Occasionally, she saw the same saint at different stages of his life. In each case, what mattered was his attitude toward God (not his earthly work as theologian, preacher, artist, or whatever). How was this attitude formed in the person, and how transparent was it? Speaking figuratively, we can say that there is fifty percent, seventy percent, and nearly one hundred percent sanctity. Where sanctity has defects, be they great or small, the fruitfulness of the mission suffers accordingly. There were also "examinations of readiness", linked with heavy penances, by which a person was tested to see how far he was willing to correspond to the increasingly harder demands of God. None of these "experiments" would have been possible in a Protestant denomination, made up of individuals. They specifically presuppose the Catholic Communion of Saints.

The fourth aspect of Adrienne's doctrine follows directly from this: her theology of ecclesial mysticism. This is fundamentally different from almost everything else that goes by the name of mysticism. Mysticism in the Catholic sense is a pure charism, given for the benefit of the Church. That is why any kind of training for mysticism is absolutely false; for Adrienne, it was an abomination.[11] In the volume *Subjektive Mystik* [Sub-

[10] N I/1–N I/2.
[11] T 2248.

jective mysticism] (1980), a theory of authentic Christian mysticism is developed, based on Old and New Testaments, which expunges the last remnants of Neo-Platonist schemes of spiritual ascent. In *Objective Mystik* [Objective mysticism] (1980), she shows that what the mystic sees, hears, experiences can never be anything but one aspect of objective revelation, upon which a clearer, more intense light is shed in order to assist the understanding of people in the present time. Much trinitarian doctrine, Christology, and ecclesiology is thereby given a new prominence or regains a forgotten relevance. There were many mystical phenomena in Adrienne's life —stigmata, transferences, the radiating of light, levitation, speaking with tongues, and other things of that kind, but they all occurred in a totally unemphatic way. They were mere accompaniments to show forth the heart of the matter: what was to be passed on to the Church, invisibly through prayer and strenuous penance, visibly through the dictated works. The criterion of her mysticism's authenticity lies primarily, if not exclusively, in the *quality* of what she did and what she had and has to say.

One final remark. All the main themes in Adrienne's work which I have here described played no role in my books before 1940, however many Church Fathers and other theologians I may have studied. If these themes emerged in my books and lectures after 1940, it is because they were taken from what I had learned from Adrienne. This will be shown briefly in what follows. At the same time, of course, my own ideas and way of thinking were not extinguished but rather enriched by what

I received from Adrienne. It is quite pointless to try to disentangle what is hers from what is mine in these later works.[12]

4. Adrienne's Help with My Work

Naturally enough, at the beginning Adrienne asked me many questions, for example, about the best way to assist at Mass. (She realized that the Mass had to be "taken as an impersonal and objective whole".)[1] But just as naturally, I asked questions of her, and, from what she had learned in prayer, she began to give me bits of advice for my relationships with people.[2] For the series of public lectures that I gave each year in Basel,[3] and for my Sunday

[12] This is where the "interweaving" of our tasks, which "in this way is willed and 'approved', becomes a reality" (T 58); cf. 325, 613, 1408 (the absolute necessity of speaking to me about her mission), 1662, 1680. Adrienne once told me that my mother, whom she had met in heaven (and who undoubtedly offered up her terminal illness and early death for my priestly vocation), had entrusted me to her (T 961).

[1] T 143.

[2] T 264.

[3] These are the lecture titles that I have been able to find: 1940/1941 —The Church as the presence of Christ. 1941/1942—God. 1942/1943 —Christ and the world. 1944/1945—The nature and forms of love. 1945/1946—Sacred scripture (God's truth in human form, a first sketch of the *Theologik* [Theo-Logic]). 1946/1947—The drama of the Christian (six lectures on plays about grace. After an introduction: Calderon's *auto, El pintor de su deshonra* [The painter of his dishonor], Shakespeare's *Measure for Measure*, Goethe's *Faust*, Strindberg's *Till Damaskus* [To Damascus], Claudel's *L'Annonce faite à Marie* [The tidings brought to Mary]. The whole series was a first sketch of the later *Theo-Drama*.) 1949/1950—Ten lectures on Karl Barth. (My book on him came out in 1951. In her prayer Adrienne was greatly concerned with K.B.) 1950/1951—The last things (the first outline of several works on eschatology, leading to *Endspiel* in 1983). 1951/1952: Mysti-

sermon in the *Marienkirche*,[4] she often gave tips and suggestions.

Most important of all was the help Adrienne gave me
during the numerous courses of the Spiritual Exercises
that I conducted, especially for students, male and female.
She never failed to prepare for these through prayer and
special penances. While they were taking place, she would
phone and make practical suggestions about how I should
deal with certain people. She would describe their appearance (she did not know the names; I had to identify them
from her descriptions) and then give a precise account of
their interior state, more often than not with instructions
on how to help them. As early as 1940: "I am praying
a great deal for the fruitfulness of these days. You can
sow the seeds of so much good there. I involve myself
as much as I can, and feel genuinely envious of those
who are actually taking part."[5] "I'm really praying for
the Exercises. Oh, there is so much I should like to give
you, to mediate to you somehow. I am thinking about
it all the time. . . ."[6] After Christmas 1942 "I phoned

---

cism. (Its definition, revelation and mysticism, Greek mysticism and
Christian mysticism, the late Middle Ages and the Catholic Refor-
mation, the modern age. I was strongly influenced here by Adrienne's
understanding of mysticism. I was already beginning to write my commentary on the questions of mysticism in St. Thomas' *Summa Theologiæ*
[2a–2æ 171–82], which was published in 1954 as volume 23 of the
German-Latin edition of St. Thomas.) In the years that followed I gave
many individual lectures, especially abroad.

[4] "Whenever I'm allowed to do something for the lectures, I constantly see the unity of our mission" (T 2052).

[5] T 47 (letter of April 4, 1941).

[6] T 183 (letter of September 24, 1941).

her from Engelberg because of a retreatant I was having some problems with. She offers herself up for the person concerned. . . . She has a very bad night."[7] In 1943 there were Exercises for women students in Mariastein. A. involved herself. The first night she slept on the floor. On the second night she asked: "May I freeze?" (She did not have any warm underclothes, and because of her many heart problems she got cold more often than she used to.) During the "Third Week" [of the Spiritual Exercises] she felt the pains of the Passion in all her limbs. During these days "she felt quite desperate about the community. Then, as already mentioned, she opened the Bible at random and found a consoling text."[8] In 1944 Adrienne again "took a great part in spirit" in the Exercises at Einsiedeln.[9] Similarly during the course in Dußnang, when she would call me daily and give me precise instructions. For individuals "she had to suffer for hours on end, and took everything on herself, in addition to the pains of Passiontide. It was a process of pull and push between life and death. She had the feeling that for the first time she knew what the Exercises were really about."[10] During a course in Stans she called me and directed me to a student I should keep an eye on.[11] There were further instructions about how to deal with young people in September that year.[12] In December, during Exercises in Engelberg, serious problems

[7] T 249.
[8] T 283–87.
[9] T 958.
[10] T 1077.
[11] T 1080.
[12] T 1171.

arose for the community. We phoned daily. A. showed me two retreatants who were not believers.[13] In the Spring of 1945 I gave another course for women students in Einsiedeln. A. gave numerous instructions, which proved to be exactly right. She did not have an hour's sleep, "but suffered the whole night for the girls. She was so much in spirit in Einsiedeln that she knew exactly whether individuals were sleeping or not, whether they were worried during the night, and so on."[14] A course I shared with Hugo Rahner in Emmetten did not at first seem to be going well. I called A. to ask for her prayers. "As it turned out, with all the hurly-burly of the journey (to Vitznau) she had not given it much thought. As soon as she began to pray, it was as if everything were turned round."[15] During a course for women students which followed shortly afterward, Adrienne had a real experience of death.[16] In July 1945 I gave the Exercises to the students who had been recently selected and organized into a training fellowship. A. pointed out "possible vocations. She often stays on her knees all night for the sake of some individual."[17] During the foundation Exercises for the women's community in Estavayer (August 1945) she once again saw "the souls of the retreatants. In one of them she saw a hidden fault that had not been confessed. Quite unobtrusively, in conversation, she got her to talk about it. Everything was all right after that." Another time she got

[13] T 1229.
[14] T 1284.
[15] T 1296.
[16] T 1298.
[17] T 1329.

into a terrible state of anxiety and trembling, and assured me that she thought she really had confessed everything. "My God, what have I hidden?" "In fact, it was one of the girls who had concealed something essential. . . ."[18] The story of this kind of cooperation could be continued at length.

Adrienne helped my work in another, very practical way. She checked proofs and read "books, about which I wanted her opinion, which always turned out to be very much to the point".[19]

There is another way in which Adrienne helped me, a form of cooperation she found much more painful: the relentless rebuking and training of her confessor. During her first Holy Week as a Catholic she was given a share in Christ's Passion. Afterward came this admission: "The hardest thing to bear was the thought that you weren't there as a friend, that you were gloating over my torment." But then suddenly this feeling that "the friend had been replaced by the observer" subsided, and she declared that my just being there, even though I was totally incapable of helping her, *had* been a help.[20] A very different scene took place on July 11, 1941. She told me to come to her office, so that—as she put it later—she could "show her contempt for me face to face". "At first I can't get a word out of her. She won't speak. This could cost our friendship." Anyway, I asked her to speak, and she did, "quietly, with a kind of ice-cold severity. It is not

---

[18] T 1346.
[19] T 765.
[20] T 53 (letter of Easter 1941).

her voice. Someone else is speaking out of her. . . . A terrifying indictment continues for almost an hour. . . . She says she is like a young mother in a labor ward. The medical students look at her and make cynical, indecent remarks. Her husband hasn't the time. He's busy somewhere else, perhaps with another woman. . . . Finally, the child arrives. He is inspected from every angle, weighed, registered. The mother nearly dies of shame. She feels violated."

She calmed down, but then the next day the recriminations became more intense. She said I was like an experienced mountaineer who has to take a young girl with him on a climb. Once out of sight, he loads his heavy rucksack onto her. "Then they begin to climb, he in ease and comfort, she with the greatest difficulty. She keeps collapsing and feels absolute terror as they pass by precipices. . . . He brusquely urges her on. He explains why it has to be like this etc., etc. Just before they reach the summit—there are people on it—he takes the rucksack back and carries it for the last few meters. Everybody is supposed to see him as the Great Guide, who can handle hard climbs, even in the company of this girl." Every word of this speech lashed me like a scourge. Somehow I pulled myself together and tried to explain that it was really in the sight of God that she was bearing my burden; it was not I but God—and at her request—who had imposed it on her. When I said this, it was as if she were waking from a dream. From deep within her, she said, "If only *that* were true!" Later she spoke about the woman's sexual role: "Carrying the child is naturally the woman's role, but the husband ought to support her and take care of her. After all, the child is his as well as hers."[21]

This experience taught me something about my responsibilities, especially when I had to discuss Adrienne's experiences with other people. Sometimes this did happen when it was not strictly necessary; each time she was aware of what was going on and criticized me for "selling her again". In most cases, though (for example, with my superiors), I just could not avoid it. So began the long and painful story of my departure from the Jesuits. The first person to object to our working together was not one of Adrienne's Protestant friends and family, but the superior of the house in which I was living.[22] By gossiping around the town, he did me more harm than anyone else.[23] To begin with, my provincial defended me against him; only when Adrienne, at my instigation, reproached him for a serious error did he begin to draw back.[24] I was then forbidden to go to the house in the *Münsterplatz* for the dictations.[25] We had to work in my office in the *Herbergsgasse*, which was very inconvenient.[26] The provincial forbad the novices I had brought into the novitiate to speak with me about Adrienne.[27] An attempt was made to turn the Bishop of Basel against me.[28] I was sent to

[21] T 121, 122.
[22] T 192.
[23] T 239, 1475.
[24] T 212, 214.
[25] T 1483.
[26] T 1498, 1509.
[27] T 1519.
[28] T 1874, 1878, 1919, 1921, 1954.

Rome for a discussion with Father General,[29] then for a second one, which decided my departure. This might have been avoided if the provincial had not dropped me.[30] Six years followed in which I was without a bishop, first in Zurich, then partly in Basel. The whole episode does not need to be described in detail here. I am mentioning it only to show the heavy responsibility that Adrienne felt for my departure from the Society; it was almost more than she could bear. (As I have said, I had forbidden her to pray for death to enable me to stay in the Society.) The sense of responsibility was all the harder because the dictations and the work we had been commanded to do together were also a source of pain. But she did all she could to lessen the burden I was carrying and to make sure that I did not notice her own. She also suffered for the Society, which I was having to leave. "The present-day Society of Jesus, like most other religious orders, is so convinced of the rightness of the form it has been given that it thinks it doesn't need to listen to the ever-present voice of God any more."[31] Adrienne's path led ever more deeply into renunciation and suffering. Before the first experience of the Passion, heaven subjected her to an agonizing test. Item by item, everything she possessed was placed in front of her, and she was asked if she would give it up.[32] Later, on a trip to Mariastein, as we were leaving a church in which we had prayed, she said: "*C'est en ordre*, It is in order." I asked what she meant.

[29] T 1707, 1759.
[30] T 1922.
[31] T 1925.
[32] T 36.

"She has now renounced her profession. She really had to tear herself away. This was the last thing chaining her to the world: the feeling of being able to do something, to achieve something earthly. But now this has been given up, or at least it will be given up."[33] In 1954, because of total infirmity and finally loss of sight, she had to give up her medical practice. However, to the very end, by her prayer and suffering, she never ceased to make my journey easier. All this she did increasingly in perceptible contact with heaven.

There is one final thing to mention in this connection, which, I have to admit, at first I simply failed to understand. In 1945 the demand was repeatedly made that "I should start a magazine". How I was to do that as a student chaplain was utterly baffling. I saw no possibility of it at all. Then came the reply: "Not now. But get on with the planning. Keep in mind the people who can write it with you."[34] Again a year later: "Don't forget the magazine!"[35] I gave it no more serious thought, even when one evening, in a cafe in the Via Aurelia in Rome, a few of us from the International Theological Commission decided to start the international review *Communio*. (It was supposed to be launched in Paris, but that fell through, so it first came out in Germany in 1973.) Even then it did not occur to me to connect this review, which now appears in eleven languages, with what I had been asked to do almost forty years earlier. Eventually the members of the founding group went their separate ways, and I

[33] T 402.
[34] T 1439.
[35] T 1643 (cf. the mention in this letter).

was left on my own and forced against my will into a kind of coordinating role. Only then did it dawn on me that there might be a connection with heaven's wish in the past. The strange blessing that rests on this fragile network linking different countries and continents confirmed me in this supposition, and imperceptibly it became a certainty.

5. From Adrienne's Letters

Some extracts from Adrienne's numerous letters—I was often away giving retreats, courses, or lectures—should make her relationship to me a little clearer. From the beginning, she saw that ours was a common endeavor. She was unable to communicate her inner experiences to anyone but me, while I had to explain much that she did not fully understand. She had, therefore, a great need for support and constant contact, as the letters written in my absence show. No exception should be taken to the way the initial *Sie* of formality for a time gives way spontaneously to the *Du* of intimacy before returning quite naturally to *Sie*. As the letters are for the most part unpublished, there is no need to supply dates; the majority of those mentioned here date from the early period after 1940.

Like all the extraordinary experiences of Adrienne (this was part of her charism as founder), what is described here has significance and consequences for the community to be formed. Those who are theologically trained, especially priests, will have to test—normally, in a much more inconspicuous way—the spiritual insights or lights of others. They must decide how these gifts are to be understood and, if need be, to bear fruit for the community and the Church.

(a) First, a few examples of how Adrienne did not fully understand many of her experiences and visions and submitted them to me for interpretation. "You see, you always give my experiences such a beautiful meaning. You understand them much better than I do. Your guidance really does make the experience meaningful and grace-filled." "I'm sorry I can't report it better, but even for me it is totally confused, completely off the beaten track, *en dehors de tout chemin tracé*. But I know that you will see the whole thing and help me. How I need your guidance! How can I ever thank you enough?" And now a very typical passage: "Until a few months ago I saw my own sins and other people's as two totally separate concepts. . . . Through what I learned from you—for which I can never be sufficiently thankful—completely different perspectives opened up. I suddenly realized—and this realization was anything but edifying—that in me there is a tendency and sometimes even a desire for every kind of sin and that, if it had depended on me, I might have committed the most incredible things in cold blood. It put everything in a totally different light. Much that till now had been in twilight or the dark showed its monstrous contours. My capacities for sin were and are unlimited. . . . This lasted for a time, then my personal sins lost their own importance, i.e., the center of gravity was shifted. Now they look like a share in the common sin of humanity as a whole. . . . My cardinal sin consists perhaps in this active participation in the general sinfulness. In and of itself, this horrible realization would have been almost unendurable had the privilege of bearing something of the sin of all not resulted from it. . . . I have described it to you in this detailed way, so that you can understand the Holy Saturday experience better. I suppose the most terrifying thing was the loss of contact between me and other beings, and that meant there was no sharing, no feeling, or not now even wish of any kind of support or help." Here Adrienne's very personal vocation of bearing burdens (which reached its most extreme form on Holy Saturday) was provoked by a theological remark about sharing in the guilt of others. But first she had to be shown the scope and meaning of this central vocation by the representative of the Church.

Another experience took place by the coffin of the twelve-year-old only child of Adrienne's greatly loved and respected friend Professor Merke. This was particularly frightening and incomprehensible and so very hard for her to bear. She had prayed "like mad" by the bed of the dying boy. She had even offered her own children to God in his place. The lad had died, and she had gone on praying, until suddenly the corpse moved and half sat up, and from heaven came a kind of voice: "Why are you going against my will?" The dead boy sank back, and the astonished nurse had to fold his hands back together. Adrienne had already performed several miracles in what one might call a trouble-free way: "At the time you always know when you have to. . . ." Now she had run into a barrier. This was a necessary learning experience, but she had to wait many days with the unendurable burden before I returned and explained things to her. Meanwhile, she described it in a letter as "the hardest thing demanded so far". "I try not to 'tremble in his hand' and am grateful for all you tell me, but the need to speak with you about everything becomes ever greater. *Tu n'as pas l'air de te rendre compte* [You don't seem to realize]."

A few more examples of Adrienne's need of explanation. I once sent her a short philosophical essay. Her response: "You know, your little philosophical *aperçu* has given me some surprising insights. When you were away, I thought: This is exactly what I have been always waiting for. Up to then I literally did not know what philosophy was. . . ." On the *Wengernalp* she read the alleged life story of Mélanie of La Salette and was deeply upset: "I believe in La Salette, of course. *Je suis payée pour le savoir* [I learned it the hard way]. But is it possible to miss the point of a mission that someone has received in this way? Tell me what you think about this possibility. In any case, it's a very serious warning for me." On her return we discussed it in detail, and later Adrienne herself, in her pictures of the saints, described this very phenomenon in numerous individual cases.

In a hotel she went each day to Mass celebrated by a priest who quite improperly made himself the center of attention. "I fought against the idea of saying separate prayers, because I wanted to take part in the *Mass*, but all my efforts were of no avail till the moment of my Communion." In the course of this it became clear "that I am completely dependent on the grace surrounding the priest. Now that is surely completely false. The Mass must be taken as an impersonal and objective whole. I fought for the whole of last week without knowing what it is. Now I see it clearly, but I can't think of any way out except to ask for your advice."

During the same vacation she had many thoughts about the community she was to found. But "some points— I guess it's because of my 'lay status'—are completely blurred for me. I note them down as points for you to decide." How could she know her way around in canon law? In this and many similar instances, it was a case of unraveling the threads which, though entangled, were in her hands and putting them in order according to Church teaching or tradition. "Right now, spiritually speaking, I can't make any kind of progress until I have spoken with you." "We mustn't be too hasty, but we must carry on— very calmly. Ultimately, of course, it is no longer our business. We are tools, and we mustn't get rusty. So I think, with your help, I should *sérieusement* [seriously] continue my education. I really must begin to work systematically, to read things and discuss them with you. You have ten years of education behind you, and I must try to pick some of it up for myself." "I *need* you, but I feel that your prayer shrouds and shelters me." "When you have finished drilling all [the students], come directly to Basel, where you are really needed . . . not everything can be done just in writing."

(b) The letters emphasize very strongly that our two missions from now on are bound together into one. Here are a few relevant texts: "Please don't say you're following my 'journey' from afar by prayer, because you know as well as I do how much you're involved in the whole thing. It was precisely your prayers which prepared the way for me into the Church. It was your human hand which again and again pulled me through my troubles. I don't want to see any reduction in the part you play. . . ." "When two people discuss together, there's always one of them who eventually declares: End of discussion. In our case I concisely and solemnly declare that I owe you a thousand times more thanks than you do me, and that ends the discussion. Your Reverence's most obedient servant, Adrienne." And again: "My deeply felt happiness cannot be repaid enough. I really am ready for every sacrifice and pray only that I can offer it up in the right way. . . . Perhaps some time or other an outward separation will come between us; I shan't worry about that. But an inward separation, as far as I am concerned, is ruled out. Forgive my boldness, but in some way you are the brother given me by God (perhaps 'brother' is too disrespectful, *pensons au sacerdoce!* [let's not forget the priesthood]). You have the most inward share in what you like to call my 'journey'. *Et d'autre part vous m'êtes très spécialement confié* [On the other hand, you have been entrusted to me in a very special way]. Thank you for the *benedictio*, thank you for your help, thank you for last year and November 1. And if the commitment can be a real and whole one, I will thank God eternally." After one Easter Sunday deliverance from the pain of the Passion: "The strange feeling I had repeatedly yesterday of having to 'explode' has completely disappeared today. I no longer feel the slightest need to speak to anyone but you about all this, but with you I want to speak a lot and in detail." "I look forward to the great and beautiful tasks which in my wildest dreams I would never have dared to assume were reserved for me, for us. Don't talk about being unworthy, because how am I supposed to describe my condition? Through your priesthood help me to serve the Lord and his Blessed Mother better." "I believe that today's [suffering], however intense, is just a prayer, perhaps our prayer. You provide the words, and I just nod and give my consent, with boundless love, a love that is glad to be 'distributed' and is permanently ready to suffer as much as God allows."

This theme is constantly repeated: "The more the 'Child' develops (that is, the idea of the community in Adrienne), the more I see how much it is *your* child." "You're right, our concerns really are common concerns." "I believe that we must pray until the way is clearly shown us, and then act. I say 'act', because I am almost certain that in this case the path is one of deeds." "Tonight I saw our Holy Father (Ignatius). He was looking at us, you and me. I was supposed to be sowing, and you were ploughing a large field. Each of us was thinking that the other one was doing the real job. Then he explained that we were only thinking this way because we couldn't see clearly enough where the division of labor came from. Then the Lord came and said: 'My blessing *is* with you', then he turned to Ignatius: 'And also with you.'" "I'd like to love and help everyone, the 'Child' and the priests, the world through him, in him. And I thank you. Now I *know* how much you are involved." "There are moments when I can clearly see that the two of us are being allowed to serve as instruments, to serve totally, and yet that means supreme happiness, albeit touched with pain." "We must both wait, because in the plan of God, who is at work in us through his Son and the Blessed Mother, there may be things that he regards as good, even though they're in fragments." "Through the very hard experiences of the last few days, a great deal seems to have been completely sealed between us. For neither of us is there the slightest possibility of turning back." Once, during the dictating of the commentary on St. John, I complained that while she was working with the full resources of the supernatural, I was taking the shorthand with only my natural capacities. She objected: "Please don't say that. The supernatural and the natural intermingle in every prayer, in all meditation. Even the one who has never had a vision cannot claim, especially in religious matters, that the interpretation comes from him. After all, he knows how dependent he is on grace, especially in interpretation, in transmission. This is just by way of setting the record straight. I am not trying to inflate my part in the commentary on John. I just want to emphasize God's part in all the religious endeavors of men."

(c) There is a third thing in the letters we should mention. It is not easy to make it comprehensible. In almost every letter Adrienne said a new Thank you, and her last words, as she died, were a repeated "Thank you, thank you, thank you." Thanks, of course, for her conversion and the graces that came to her through it, but chiefly for keeping company with her in her dark nights of Godforsakenness. The person standing by could not bring any kind of light into this darkness laid upon her by God. And yet someone had to be there, even though from time to time his presence was felt as more or less a nuisance, because he confronted her experience without knowledge, as happening to someone else, seemingly as a mere observer. Only afterward did the fact that someone was there appear as consoling and encouraging. "It fills me with happiness to think that you helped me so much to carry on through that night [of Good Friday]. Your help will become more intelligible to me as the days go by. I guess I felt it momentarily even at the time, but only now do I appreciate its value." "You know, later and at certain moments even while it's happening, it is a great relief for you to be there. I had a place where I could lay my head, and despite the terrors a great deal of good stays with me from those long hours, good that was given me through your presence. I'm looking forward to you being there, so we can discuss the whole thing together, sometime when we have a few peaceful hours, with the Gospels in our hands. I'm longing to read the Passion. I can't think it through on my own. It's all still so recent."

There were also interior dark nights when I was absent. Then she tried to communicate at least something of it to me in her letters. On the one hand, she was looking forward to a discussion that would explain it to her, but on the other hand, she wanted to assure me that I was included in her suffering of the Passion. "The night was anxious, and the day remains night, seemingly eternal, without beginning or end. Now and then a *Suscipe* is said, *quasi in memoriam*, while the enticing temptations of flight are just a sign of total abandonment. Every opening is a grille. An impenetrable wall would be more human.

And it's strange, that 'human' is not actually a synonym of 'sinful'. Is it still prayer when you call out and cry 'Crush me, let my whole soul become a single wound, if only it be in thy name?' I don't know any more. When, roughly, are you coming to Basel?" "Being alone like this is humanly speaking almost unbearably hard. And yet again and again it is noticeably eased by the fact that you know of my existence and also share in it—and not just by your understanding and sympathy. For that, once again, thank you." "Help me to stay in 'jail' and to surrender everything, yes everything, to him."

"I'd like to say something about our conversation today. Of course, I don't think you should pray for me to have no more anxiety, because I know well enough that I am going to meet much more anxiety, anxiety that penetrates the very marrow, and that it really is part of the Cross. But I do ask you by your prayers to help me not to be frightened of anxiety. Help me not to neglect any of the things I have to do, so I don't try to avoid feeling the extremes of anxiety. You know that I really do want to say Yes to everything. Now and then I am frightened when new perspectives open up, but I belong totally to the Lord, and I thank you for having led me to him." On one occasion after a long vacation: "*Je tacherai d'être raisonnable* [I shall strive to be reasonable], but once again it has been such a long period of separation, and I have been wandering so long in the fog that soon I really shall need you to shake me out of myself."

Especially hard was the sudden, totally unexpected stigmatization. This made her feel extremely ashamed and plunged her into terrible anxiety. Once again she sought refuge with her confessor. "Something human is involved here, something which must, which *wants*, to be protected. There may be no word to describe this, but I am sure of it, and I think you are too." Then she speaks of certain words: "I wasn't really thinking about them. They were poured into me, though that's not quite right —I uttered them, maybe in a low voice, so that I could be conscious of where they came from. Something like this: *'Je veux essayer de faire tout ce que tu voudras, et nous voulons tous deux t'aimer, te servir et te remercier de "l'Église que tu nous confie"* [I want to try to do all you will, and we both want to love you, to serve you, and to thank you for "the Church you are entrusting to us"].' This last phrase was suddenly spoken and dictated by the Mother of God. I mean that the two of us spoke it together, and suddenly, for a split second, she put the Child (our child, remember) into my arms, but it was no longer just the Child. It was the *Una Sancta* in miniature. I think this gives a real unity to everything we have been asked to do. In God we're working on the *Catholica*."

Here Adrienne herself provides the interpretation; at other times she asks me to help her understand. "It's like this: you have a lamp in your hand and know the path, while I can only feel the hardness of the cobbles and don't realize that this hardness is just part of the path." Occasionally, before going into the night, she can see the coming day behind it, and then she asks for my prayers: "There's a splendor behind the dark and threatening cloud. It's as if the edge of the cloud were golden, promising what lies behind. And yet I don't know that the path leads *through* the cloud, and once I'm inside it nothing more can be seen of the golden edge. Help me to pray for obedience, when I'm completely inside. The cloud isn't very thick."

There is this account of a walk through the *Bahnhof-straße* in Zurich, on the way back to Basel. "Discouraged by the 'life without God' of the people streaming past, but then encouraged by the very strong feeling that he is constantly accompanying me and struck by the thought that his work, the need to make him known, is not just a remote necessity, but somehow also an immediate demand. And suddenly I knew. For a moment it was almost liberating, really liberating, but then, in the course of the next few hours, it became an oppressive burden: no one and nothing is as close to you and me as he is. This isn't madness, obsession. *C'est tout simplement la réalité* [It's quite simply reality]. He is there. We are his work and the instrument of his work, and only his mission counts. . . . We have to do it, but how can we if we don't want to? . . . *Expropriation complète* [complete expropriation], *Suscipe omnia* [Take, Lord, everything]. Everything else is just a vague hint, a feeble attempt, a children's game compared with the immensity of the lack of love. Lord, give us love, only love, so that we can serve you. Yours in deepest distress, Adrienne."

(d) For the sake of balance I must add that her gratitude for my support and occasionally for theological help did not prevent her from giving me severe warnings as we went along. Here are a few examples: "You shouldn't be involved so intensely. You should sleep and be thankful. You are thankful, of course, but you should sleep and rest, so that these few days of vacation will bear fruit." "Please have a proper rest. You need it, and you mustn't produce books nonstop."

"May I say something painful, though I mean it kindly? When I read what you have written . . . , I sometimes feel you are writing for a totally theoretical person, in other words, for someone who lives only in your mind, a person who has all your presuppositions, who always *à demi* [half] shares your understanding, and this person simply does not exist. So I think it would be good for you to get to know the 'normal' man. Somehow you must be brought through him to him. . . . You can't write just for the sake of the subject matter. You have to do it for the reader." "I'm thinking a great deal about your 'Church'. Isn't this the great temptation for you? To create a monument for yourself rather than for him? I don't know. It just seems to me that right now you aren't in any way ready for a really great undertaking. The Child is certainly developing and will sap your strength. . . . [There is] no limit to the things we have not chosen, the things that make you, like me, want to cry out 'No!' We're just not consulted. You may want to write the great book in thirty years' time. Well and good, but what else are you going to do?" "Of course, it would be good if you didn't work so frightfully hard. For these few days before the semester begins, can't you be just a tiny bit less cerebral?" And when she reads *Das Herz der Welt* [*The Heart of the World*]: "You know, there are some passages at the beginning that I find a little weak. In other words, your pleasure in playing with a word, its sound, its structure, its connotations, seems now and then almost to obscure the spiritual content. I'd be glad . . . to note it down, if it would be helpful to you."

This does not mean that Adrienne regarded my writing with suspicion. There was much to which she showed a positive attitude. During the early years in Basel I took over the "Klosterberg Collection" for a Protestant publisher. The series was intended as an introduction to the great classics of European literature. To begin with, Adrienne had a lot of misgivings about such a waste of time, but then she realized that a series like this was a way of reaching out to many people outside the Church, and so she dropped her objections.

These critical remarks of Adrienne are a good way of leading into the next section, which will be concerned with my literary output from 1940 onward.

6. My Works since 1940

I must now describe as briefly as possible the spiritual part played by Adrienne in what I have written since I first met her. This is not an easy task. The views and projects I brought with me are so interconnected with what came from her that the two can never be neatly separated. Still, certain things are clear.

I have already mentioned the works I had written before 1940. I have explained how Adrienne's experiences bolstered my chief interests (in St. Irenaeus, Origen, St. Gregory of Nyssa, and St. Maximus the Confessor), answered unresolved questions, and confirmed the correctness of what I was trying to do.[1]

[1] With regard to St. Irenaeus and his interior attitude, see the highly

Das Herz der Welt [*The Heart of the World*] (written in 1943) is the first direct echo of my involvement with Adrienne's Paschal experiences—the Eastertide and eucharistic experiences as well as those of Good Friday and Holy Saturday. The lyrical, hymn-like style of the book is not appropriate to her own, which was always very plain and down-to-earth. It is a sign of my enthusiasm and sense of wonder at these privileged insights into the mystery of Christ in all its fullness. Much seen here is repeated later in more objective form. The chapter on the descent into hell is directly dependent on Adrienne's Holy Saturday experiences, as are all the later references to this mystery, which have already been mentioned above: the passage in *Die Gottesfrage des heutigen Menschen* [The God-question of modern man; English translation: *Science, Religion, and Christianity*] (1956), the various essays on eschatology (in *Theologie heute* [Theology today], ed. L. Reinisch, 1959, in *Verbum Caro* [*Word Made Flesh*] (1960), in *Pneuma und Institution* [Spirit and institution] (1974), *Mysterium Paschale* (in *Mysterium Salutis* III, 1969), and the final volume of *Theodramatik* [*Theo-Drama*] (1983).

The fragment *Wahrheit. Ein Versuch* I: Wahrheit der Welt [Truth. An essay I: The truth of the world] (1947) grew out of lectures that I gave to the Students' Training Fellowship, which I founded with Robert Rast. It falls

informative supplement in T 1401–2. For Origen, see the vision in T 1626. T 2086 reveals the special bond between him and Adrienne. I have already mentioned that Adrienne's theology of confession confirms what I was trying to do in *Apokalypse der deutschen Seele* (1937–39).

back on what I had learned earlier in philology (Goethe's and Christian von Ehrenfels' understanding of *Gestalt* as expression and of the need to see things as wholes) and philosophy (in first place, St. Thomas). This book was meant to serve as a foundation for the more important second book, *Wahrheit Gottes* [The truth of God], which would articulate much of what came from Adrienne. In an un-Thomistic way, I put the Beautiful (the marvel of being and the response of astonishment to it) before the Good and the True. This anticipates the plan of my later trilogy, which begins with an Aesthetic (the Beautiful), continues with a Dramatic (the Good), and concludes with the Theologic (the True), which, practically speaking, ought to form the second volume of *Wahrheit* I (at this time still unwritten). The theological concept of truth should be unfolded here. (I am thinking of St. John's doctrine of truth, which has been expounded by Father Ignace de la Potterie, S.J., but which is also Adrienne's constant presupposition.) In this area of interest one might also include all the attempts to bring Goethe's views into the realm of theology: *Einfaltungen* [*Convergences*] (1969), *Die Wahrheit ist symphonisch* [*Truth Is Symphonic*] (1972), *Christen sind einfältig* [Christians are simple] (1983).

Der Laie und der Ordensstand [The layman and the religious state] (1948) is the first and rather inadequate prospectus for what will be described below as Adrienne's and my most important concern: a community for women and men who live and work in the world but at the same time follow the evangelical counsels. A good many of the essays in *Skizzen zur Theologie* [*Explo-*

rations in Theology] have developed the theme. A group
of experts called together by Pope Paul VI enabled me
(in a subcommission dealing with secular institutes for
priests) for the first time to come to grips with this subject. In the form which our "Community of St. John" is
finally taking, the priests' branch will play an important
role alongside the lay men and women. Our publishing
house brought out a Latin-German edition of the chief
papal documents on secular institutes (1963).

Thérèse von Lisieux: Geschichte einer Sendung [*Thérèse of
Lisieux: The Story of a Mission*] (1950) would never have
come about without Adrienne's theology of mission. She
was deeply preoccupied with the saints, but she also gave a
critical account of their spiritual journeyings[2] and shifted
emphasis away from psychology toward theology. I built
on all this in my study, which decked out the insights
taken from Adrienne with a rich array of texts from St.
Thérèse. The shorter work *Elisabeth von Dijon und ihre
geistliche Sendung* [*Elizabeth of Dijon and her Spiritual Mission*] (1952) is complementary to the one on Thérèse.
Here the move from the story of the saint's life to her
theological mission was much easier to make. With the
help of two great figures, Mary of Jesus and Father Vallée,
O.P., Elizabeth attained a theological objectivity which
it is hard to find in the saint of Lisieux, who was forced
into thinking about herself. Elizabeth's discovery of the
biblical meaning of "predestination" is also quite amazing. This revives much of Origen's thinking and includes
insights that we find in Adrienne. It is a counterpart to

[2] In *Allerheilegenbuch* [The book of all saints] I/2, 64–88.

Thérèse's discovery of a total hope. These two figures—poles apart, yet mutually complementary—were eventually brought together in *Schwestern im Geist* [*Two Sisters in the Spirit*] (4th ed. 1990).

The first version of my book *Christlicher Stand* [*The Christian State of Life*] was written in about 1945. My provincial advised me not to publish it. He thought the doctrine of "call", based on the first contemplation of the second week of the *Spiritual Exercises*, was too complicated. It appeared in a revised version in 1977, but only some chapters in the middle of the book had been changed. The introductory reflections on Paradise are influenced by the Fathers (especially St. Gregory of Nyssa) and similar ideas of Adrienne. The concluding part seems to me to be in line with the recommendations of the Exercises. Adrienne's doggedly maintained opinion about the "two states" (marriage and the counsels—there is no third way)[3] also left its mark on the study. The final version tries to situate the priestly office among the states of Christian life and thus, like Adrienne, to demonstrate the convergence between the priesthood and the life of the counsels.[4]

Theologie der Geschichte [*The Theology of History*] (1950,

---

[3] "There is no third state" (T 1935; cf. T 1953, 2204, 2338 [the foolish virgins and the "third state"]). Adrienne's book with the same name (dictated in 1949, published in 1956) contains some very enriching theological ideas: "state" in the Trinity (cf. T 2198); Christ as the mediator of the heavenly state in his "readiness to serve God and his creation of a relationship to the world" (163); the Church and her relationship to Christ embracing the Christian states of life and leading them back to herself (173).

[4] Cf. T 1883; cf. I/2, 284–86.

the new edition of 1959 is the definitive one), like the collection of essays *Das Ganze im Fragment: Aspekte der Geschichtstheologie* [The whole in the fragment: Aspects of the theology of history] (2d ed. 1990), contains much that is my own. It is indebted in part to Henri de Lubac (for example, the dialogue with Teilhard de Chardin) and to the suggestions of Ferdinand Ulrich (for example, what I say about St. Augustine's doctrine of time). However, the consistent centering on Christ, especially the doctrine of the "Forty Days", the idea of the universalizing of the Christ-event by the Holy Spirit, and the doctrine of mission and the Christian tradition are clearly inspired by Adrienne.[5] The theme of the "time of Christ", which I touched upon here, was first properly developed in "Zuerst Gottes Reich" [Seek ye first the kingdom of God] (1966). With the theme of mission (*missio* as the economic form of *processio*), it became the center of the Christology of *Theodramatik* [*Theo-Drama*] II/2 (1978), III (1980), and IV (1983). The chapter "Man as the Speech of God" was first published in *Verbum Caro* [*Word Made Flesh*] (1960) and then considerably widened and deepened. It is bound up with the question I considered when trying to interpret Adrienne: How can divine truth be "adequately" translated into human (existential and conceptual) truth? The *Theologik* [Theo-Logic] will take this question up again.[6]

[5] For the Forty Days, see T 307, 2141–42, 2355. The other themes can be found scattered throughout Adrienne's biblical commentaries.

[6] On the stages of the life of the Word made flesh, see *Das Ganze im Fragment* [The whole in the fragment] (268ff.). Cf. the provocative ideas of St. Irenaeus, *Adversus Hæreses* II, 22, 4 and III, 18, 7.

The book *Karl Barth* (6th ed. 1989)[7] is the fruit of numerous conversations with the man himself. (Adrienne supported these with intensive prayer and works of penance.) Barth's dialogue with Erich Przywara had broken down ("*Analogia entis* as Antichrist"). I wanted to get things moving again and clear away some of the chief obstacles in ecumenical dialogue by using ideas from de Lubac's *Surnaturel* [Supernatural] and *Sur les chemins de Dieu* [On the pathways of God]. I was tremendously and lastingly attracted by Barth's doctrine of election, that brilliant overcoming of Calvin. It converged with Origen's views and therefore with Adrienne's Holy Saturday theology as well. Barth was very interested in Adrienne's conversion and asked me about the reasons for it. He "is very pensive".[8]

Der Christ und die Angst [The Christian and anxiety] (6th ed. 1989) came from two influences. First, there were the preoccupations of Georges Bernanos, especially his stage adaptation of Gertrud von Le Fort's "Die Letzte am Schafott" [The last one on the scaffold; English translation: *Song at the Scaffold*], but also his *Diary of a Country Priest*. The importance of these works was brought home to me in a new way by Albert Béguin, whom I had received into the Church shortly after Adrienne (she was his godmother). Secondly, and of course even more significantly, there were Adrienne's experiences of supernatural anxiety. She repeatedly declared that "for her these states of anxiety were the strangest thing of all. . . . Before her conversion, she says, she had a very stable temperament.

[7] Written much earlier. Cf. T 162.
[8] T 255.

She had always been a lively and enterprising person. She had never been afraid of anything. She didn't recognize herself any more."[9] St. Ignatius felt the same surprise at himself in Manresa.[10] Her dark nights were to be marked by an extreme anxiety, which was imposed upon her and reached the very edge of insanity. She very often asked for these nights so she could make reparation. When they were over, her natural, anguish-free character reappeared. My essay tries to put the phenomenon of the anxiety of sin in the context of salvation history, from Wisdom chapter 17 and the Apocalypse to our Lord's agony in the garden and the various ways in which Christians follow him in that agony in experiences both normal and extraordinary.

Schleifung der Bastionen [*Razing the Bastions*] (5th ed. 1989) has often been regarded as an anticipation of the *aggiornamento* thinking of Pope John XXIII. I am supposed to have retracted it all after the Council and taken up a conservative position. In fact, the origins of the book are quite different. It is concerned with the universality of salvation,[11] as proposed by Origen, E. Przywara, H. de Lubac, and K. Barth, and examined by me in *Theologie der Geschichte* [*The Theology of History*]. Adrienne's concept of

---

[9] T 853.

[10] "Up to this time he continued undisturbed in the same interior state." When desolation begins to descend upon him, he asks: "What kind of new life is this that we are now beginning?" (*A Pilgrim's Journey: The Autobiography of Ignatius of Loyola*, English translation: Joseph N. Tylenda, S.J. [Wilmington, 1985], 29f.).

[11] Joseph Ratzinger realized this quite correctly. See his "Christlicher Universalismus. Zum Aufsatzwerk H. U. v. Balthasars", *Hochland* 54 (1961): 68–76.

mission, applied to the Church sent into and open toward
the world, outlined the same thing. In my work in this
area of discussion, there are no retractions of any sort. On
the contrary, there is a direct line of continuity right up
to the little books *In Gottes Einsatz leben* [*Engagement with
God*] (2d ed. 1972) and *Katholisch* [English translation: *In
the Fullness of Faith*] (2d ed. 1975). *Schleifung der Bastionen*
is also a kind of homage to my teachers E. Przywara and
H. de Lubac as well as to Adrienne von Speyr. All three of
them showed me, in contrast to a narrow scholastic theology, the world-spanning dimensions of what is Catholic.

I have composed frequent variations on the theme of
Theologie und Heiligkeit [Theology and holiness].[12] Without doubt, the first stimulus for it came from the theology of the Church Fathers. However, sharing in the life
of Adrienne was the immediate cause of my giving new
expression to this desire for theology and holiness to be
one. This woman doctor united the two in a unique and
almost unfathomable way.

Closely connected with these issues is the book on
Bernanos (1954). What concerns this writer in all his
fiction is the phenomenon of sanctity lived out in the
Church—whether by the priest, whom he considers as
exemplary, or by a layperson such as Chantal in "Joy",
the vicarious sacrificial lamb immolated by the evil men
who surround her. When I say "Church" here, I give the
word the very objective and Catholic meaning it had for
Bernanos: a Church of the (lived!) sacraments and the

---

[12] First in *Wort and Wahrheit* 3 (1948), then in *Verbum Caro* [*Word
Made Flesh*] (1960). Cf. Adrienne's short treatise about asceticism and
theology (T 2214).

obedience of office. Haunted by the extreme evil that can be committed by men, Bernanos writes on the very edge of hell's abyss. And yet hell for him is again and again infiltrated and held in check by the devoted Christians who follow Christ in suffering and powerlessness. Few books have I written with more interior involvement than this one, which I worked on immediately after leaving the Jesuits.

Reinhold Schneider: Sein Weg und sein Werk [Reinhold Schneider: His way and his work] (1953 = *Nochmals: Reinhold Schneider* 1991) has a somewhat different center. This writer's works—prose and drama—are constantly preoccupied with the confrontation of the saint with the Christian who has temporal power at his command—emperor, king or Pope. This theme, which, for Schneider, usually has a tragic resolution (the rift between the world and the Kingdom of God can only be closed in the Cross of Christ), is something which a person in a secular institute also has to confront. How can his obedience to God and the Church be compatible with his obedient responsibilities in his secular profession? In all the years Adrienne and I spent thinking about how to live consistently in a secular institute, this issue never lost its topicality, as can be seen from the paper I gave at the First International Congress of Secular Institutes in Rome in 1971, which, needless to say, did not go unchallenged.[13] Numerous attempts to describe the form of life in a secular institute followed through the years.[14]

---

[13] *Acta primi Congressus Internat. Institutorum sæcularium*, September 20–26 (Rome, 1971), 1024–32.

[14] Apart from the slim volume already mentioned *Der Laie und der Or-*

Thomas von Aquin. Besondere Gnadengaben [St. Thomas Aquinas: Special graces] (a commentary on the *Summa Theologiæ* 2a–2æ, qq. 171–82, vol. 23, in the Latin-German edition of the *Summa*, 1954) had its source entirely in my experience of the charismatic gifts of Adrienne. The concrete form these took led me to criticize the thesis held by St. Thomas that the exercise of a charism (in the sense of a *gratia gratis data*) does not require the state of sanctifying grace. Of course, St. Thomas himself knew that to live out a charism for any length of time and in any adequate way is impossible without grace. Old Testament examples (such as Balaam) were the reason for the Scholastic thesis.

I wrote *Das betrachtende Gebet* [(Contemplative) Prayer;

---

densstand [The layman and the religious state] (1948), see, in *Hans Urs von Balthasar: Bibliographie 1925–1990* (Einsiedeln: Johannes Verlag, 1990), B 71 (The trouble with lay orders), B 89 (World, orders, secular orders), B 95 (The secular office of the laity), B 102 (The nature and scope of secular institutes), B 108 (On the theology of secular institutes), B 122 (New forms of community in today's Church), B 145 (Theological aspects of profession), B 169 (The evangelical counsels in the Catholic Church of today), B 178 (The gospel as critical norm for every form of spirituality in the Church), B 194 (Secular spirituality?), B 241 ([In the world, but not of the world], which comes from *Das Wagnis der Nachfolge* [The risk of following him], ed. S. Richter [1964], where it appears under the title, [The theology of the state of the evangelical counsels]), B 247 (Life that is ready for God), B 254 (On the theology of the religious vows), B 274 (Celibate existence today), B 286 (The paradox of secular institutes), B 328 (Existence as mission), B 362 (In the frontier zone of the laity), in *Internationale katholische Zeitschrift Communio* (1981) 238–45 (The risk of the secular institutes). See also *Gottbereites Leben*, vol. I: *Der Laie und der Rätestand*; vol. II: *Nachfolge Christi in der heutigen Welt* (Einsiedeln, Freiburg: Johannes Verlag, 1993.)

English translation: *Prayer*] (1955) because I realized that it was impossible to find any introduction to such prayer that was not merely ascetical and spiritual but built upon the truly biblical foundation of hearing the Word of God. Once again, the suggestive ideas and example of the Fathers were in the background, but the immediate source of inspiration was Adrienne's scriptural exegesis. Taken as a whole, this was nothing other than a hearing and contemplating of God's Word in Old and New Testaments. (The capacity to hear was, admittedly, bestowed on her in a quite unique way, and the contemplation was as much infused as acquired.) What was set forth here as a kind of model and forerunner had to be reproduced in the ordinary framework of every Christian's prayer, especially that of the Community of St. John. In the years that followed, many articles developed the basic ideas of this book. I had a plan for a series—the *Adoratio* collection—which, in line with this program, would have opened up the various books of the Bible for contemplative prayer. It fell through because of a lack of collaborators. I tried to make a start on this in my book *Thessalonicher- und Pastoralbriefe für das betrachtende Gebet erschlossen* [The Epistles to the Thessalonians and the Pastoral Epistles opened up for contemplative prayer] (3d ed. 1993), and Adrienne's points for meditation on St. Mark's Gospel (1971) also fits into the plan.

Many of my minor works can be passed over here, such as *König David* [King David] (1955), *Die Gottesfrage des heutigen Menschen* [The God-question of modern man] (1956), which grew out of lectures (I mentioned it above because of its chapter on the descent into hell), the books on Buber, *Einsame Zwiesprache. Martin Buber und das Christentum* (2d ed. 1993) [English translation: *Martin Buber and Christianity.* Harvill Press, London/New York, Macmillan Company, 1961] and Guardini, *In Gottes Einsatz leben* [*Engagement with God*] (2d ed. 1972, written for Luigi Giussani's movement), the works on the unity of theology and pluralism in theology and the Church (*Einfaltungen* [*Convergences*] [4th ed. 1988], *Die Wahrheit ist symphonisch* [*Truth is Symphonic*] [1972]), the books written to help unsettled Christians (*Klarstellungen* [*Elucidations*] [4th ed. 1978], *Neue Klarstellungen* [*New Elucidations*] [3d ed. 1989], *Kleine Fibel für verunsicherte Laien* [*A Short Primer for Unsettled Laymen*] [1980], *Christen sind einfältig* [Christians are simple] [1983]). These, too, of course, have many features that go back more or less directly to Adrienne.

By way of conclusion, here are a few central themes which reveal the common task.

In 1960 I began to plan a trilogy, of which *Herrlichkeit* [*The Glory of the Lord*] (1961–1969) is the first part. It takes up the idea of the "wonder" in being which I discussed in *Wahrheit* I [Truth I] (see above), but from the outset it was focused on the Johannine understanding of glory as uniting both the Cross and Resurrection of Jesus. In the Cross and Resurrection, the glory of the triune God shines forth in a unique and unmistakable way. In 1948 Adrienne succinctly summed up the mystery as follows: "The Incarnation of the Son does not diminish his glory. On the contrary, it accentuates it, but it does so through a giving up, a renouncing of his glory. It would be quite false to think that, during the time of this giving up, the Father and the Holy Spirit had to hold on to their glory all the more tightly. Clearly, the whole Godhead is involved in this giving up by the Son. We are talking here about an act and attitude of the whole Godhead. Man has been entrusted by God with the commandment of solidarity—especially when one member is suffering. It would surely be very strange if the author of that commandment dispensed himself from it."[15] Many passages in Adrienne's commentary on St. John's Gospel circle around this mystery of triune glory revealing itself in the destiny of Christ.[16] Just one quotation may be sufficient proof that the central Johannine outlook of my entire work is in harmony with Adrienne's writing on St. John. The second volume of *Herrlichkeit* [English translation: *The Glory of the Lord* II and III] (the twelve theologians who focus on the mystery of glory and make a "systematics" impossible) and the third volume [*The Glory of the Lord* IV and V] (the philosophical foundations

---

[15] T 2011.

[16] Vol. 1, 418; vol. 2, 60, 250–51: Jesus as "the glory of the Father himself", who for his part "seeks the glory of the Son" (432); the objective seeing of Jesus' glory by Martha (vol. 3, 402); the Son's possession of the whole glory of the Father and his returning of it to the Father (484); the glory of the Son is one with his holiness, which abandons itself to the darkness of sin, and "so he places his own on the dividing line between the glory of the Father and the sin of mankind" (485–86); Jesus' self-abandonment is his "transparency" to the whole glory of God's love—he is "pure openness". "Certainly, [God] remains mysterious and beyond our reckoning, but he is not like an opaque mystery that one cannot get behind. No, he is mysterious in the boundlessness and openness of his mystery." This very sentence is paraphrased in my little book *Christen sind einfältig* [Christians are simple] (1983), in which I contend with philosophical negative theology.

of the experience of being as "wonder") are indeed the fruit of my theological study, but everything leads into a theology of the Cross which is in perfect conformity to Adrienne's. At this point mention should be made of the short programmatic work *Glaubhaft ist nur Liebe* (5th ed. 1985) [English translation: *Love Alone: The Way of Revelation* (5th ed. 1992)]. Only Adrienne's Christology, which gets beyond every kind of *apokatastasis* doctrine, can justify this daring title. Any attempt to have access to the ultimate mystery without Christ is ruled out. The *Endspiel* [The final act] (*Theodramatik* [*Theo-Drama*] IV), with its chapter on the pain of God, should be fitted into the same context.

One other important thing must be emphasized. Aesthetics, in the sense of the doctrine of the beautiful, has its starting point in a distinction between two elements "which have traditionally controlled every aesthetic, and which, with Thomas Aquinas, we could term *species* (or *forma*) and *lumen* (or *splendor*)—form [*Gestalt*] and splendor [*Glanz*]. . . . Form would not be beautiful unless it were fundamentally a sign and appearing of a depth and a fullness that, in themselves and in an abstract sense, remain beyond both our reach and our vision."[17] This key sentence applies not only to every manifestation of spirit in body in this world but also to the most profound manifestation of God in salvation history, the manifestation of God in his Son in human form. Without knowing anything about aesthetics, Adrienne, in her brilliant little book *Das Licht und die Bilder: Elemente der Kontemplation*

[17] *Herrlichkeit* I, 111; English translation: *The Glory of the Lord* I, 118.

[The light and the images: Elements of contemplation] (2d ed. 1986), works along the same lines and, in the process, has given us one of the most concentrated accounts of Christian contemplation ever written. It expels all Neo-Platonizing hostility to images, and it does so in the name of the images created for us by God, but above all in the name of him whom creation images, God's incarnate Son. We cannot get beyond his bodiliness, because it is the very means by which all the light of God's love is communicated to us.[18]

The second part of my trilogy, the *Theodramatik* [*Theo-Drama*] (1973-1983), to put it briefly, is based first of all on the concept of mission, which gives a higher and more complete meaning to the Christian and psychological notion of "role" (cf. the theatrical analogies for human existence in antiquity and the Baroque period). Secondly, it is concerned with the confrontation of finite creaturely freedom with infinite divine freedom. Mission is presented here as the central concept of Christology and the following of Christ. It is in harmony with the whole Ignatian and Johannine theology of Adrienne. The confrontation, which in its most extreme form is between divine freedom and antidivine demonic freedom, became as dramatic and concrete in Adrienne's life as it was for St. Anthony the Great, the Curé of Ars, and

---

[18] My last attempt to give, in summary form, an anti-Platonic account of what Christian mysticism was "Christian Mysticism Today" in *Der Weg zum Quell: Festschrift Teresa von Avila* [The way to the spring: a festschrift for St. Teresa of Avila] (Patmos, 1982), 11-51. On Adrienne's understanding of mysticism, see the brief section in T 1289 and the more detailed treatment in *Subjektive Mystik* (Einsiedeln, 1980).

Don Bosco. The "thesis" of mission-obedience to God
had to pass the searing test of taking on the "antithesis".
This was unending and pushed to the outer limits of
endurance.[19]

My writings about *Mary and the Church* can also be
classified under the heading of the concept of mission
(which is the same thing as theological person). At the
foot of the Cross, Mary shared the suffering of her Son
and was handed over by him to John, thus becoming the
"Church" (in the Church's innermost being as Bride of
Christ). This is Adrienne's constant teaching.[20] In an article (which Father Congar found "obscure") I tried to
use the concept of Mary's mission (particular and univer-

---

[19] *A propos* of the *Theodramatik*, there is another question to be considered. As a theological issue, it constantly preoccupied me in connection with Adrienne's experience of suffering. Her extreme states of
suffering (such total darkness, so overtaxing, that she would be on the
point of giving everything up, the experience of eternal damnation,
etc.) were the result of having joyfully offered herself up to suffering. Beneath all the world's suffering, even the most desperate, should
there not be a kind of joy (albeit no longer felt)? Adrienne said as
much many times (T 1992, 2157, 2148). I repeated the same point in
"Das Tragische und der christliche Glaube" [The tragic and Christian faith] (in *Hochland* 57 [1965]), "Die Freude und das Kreuz" [Joy
and the Cross] (in *Concilium* IV [1968]), also in *Die Wahrheit ist symphonisch* [*Truth Is Symphonic*] [1972]), "Die Abwesenheiten Jesu" [The
absences of Jesus] (in *Geist und Leben* 44 [1971], also in *Die Wahrheit ist
symphonisch* [1972]). This leads to a more carefully considered theology
of substitution, which is nowadays being explored in new ways by a
great diversity of people.

[20] In addition to numerous passages in the commentaries: T 2175
(Mary as *Catholica*), why Mary shows herself (T 1821), Mary as the
fulfillment of all the faith of the Old Testament (*Achtzehn Psalmen*
[Eighteen Psalms], 41).

sal) to show her meaning for the whole Church ("Who Is the Church?").[21] The same scene at the foot of the Cross helps us understand how Mary-Church is not only offered with Christ but also offers with him.[22] I show this in my essay "The Mass: An Offering of the Church?"[23] By the Cross, Mary (and in her the other Marys of the Gospel) plays "the role of the Church". She does this in her connection with John,[24] without prejudicing office, which is primarily personified in Peter. This is the background for understanding my highly condensed answer to the pretensions of feminist theology (in the article "The Dignity of Woman").[25] My many publications about the

---

[21] In *Sponsa Verbi* (Einsiedeln, 2d ed. 1971), 148–202; English translation: *Spouse of the Word*: Explorations in Theology II (San Francisco: Ignatius Press, 1991), 143–92. Also in the Herder Library 239 (1965): *Wer ist die Kirche?* [Who is the Church?] (four essays).

[22] In an account of Adrienne's view of the Mass, it says: "At the oblation, A. in the Spirit sees the Church: her foundation by the Lord, her power to have him at her disposal." The priest is now "a pure representative of the Church. *She* offers the Sacrifice. . . . It is a question not just of the gift on the altar but of the will of the faithful to let themselves be offered up at the same time. It is as if no one has the right to be if he is not willing to share in the action" (T 1640). Cf. *Die heilige Messe* [Holy Mass] (1980): "To offer meaningfully and validly is always to offer with the sacrificial attitude of the Son, who lives in us, in whose offering we join. This offering is made first of all by the priest. . . . He, the priest, is included in the mystery of this offering . . . because he has offered himself, so that he can offer it. His personal offering is presupposed and taken up into the oblation that has been prepared" (49).

[23] In *Spiritus Creator* (2d ed. 1988), 166–217; English translation: *Creator Spirit*: Explorations in Theology III.

[24] Cf. the commentary on John 19:26–27.

[25] "Die Würde der Frau", in *Internationale katholische Zeitschrift: Communio* 11 (1980), 346–52.

Mother of the Lord need not be individually listed here,[26] except for *Der antirömische Affekt* [English translation: *The Office of Peter*] (2d ed. 1989), which presents Mary as embodying the Church in an all-embracing way, while the male "pillars"—Peter-John and Paul-James (office, love, freedom, tradition)—stand for the inner structure of the Church in the tensions of her unity.

The John-Peter grouping called for a corresponding vigorous theology of ministry, especially of *priestly spirituality*. The disappointment Adrienne felt with many of the secular priests she met and her ceaseless support for them by works of penance inspired my writings on this subject. These writings promoted the theology of celibacy, and of the evangelical counsels in general, for the diocesan clergy without trying to turn them into religious.[27]

---

[26] See above all my meditations on the Rosary, which seek to put Mary back in the general context of the order of salvation: *Der dreifache Kranz: Das Heil der Welt im Mariengebet* [*The Threefold Garland: The World's Salvation in Mary's Prayer*] [3d ed. 1979] (in the series *Beten heute* [*Praying Today*] 9). See also the book I wrote with Joseph Cardinal Ratzinger, *Maria—Kirche im Ursprung* [Mary—the original Church] (Herder, 1980). On how all the missions in the Church are contained within the all-embracing mission of Mary, see *Der antirömische Affekt* (2d ed. 1989) [*The Office of Peter*] and "Die marianische Prägung der Kirche" ["The Marian character of the Church"] (in *Maria heute ehren* [Devotion to Mary today], Herder [1977]), 263–79.

[27] Cf. in the *Bibliographie 1925–1990*: C 27 (Person and function), B 208 (On the priestly office), B 231 (Ministerial priesthood and the people of God), B 233 (The priest in the New Testament), B 256 (The priest in the Church), B 258 (On the question of the priest at the episcopal synod 1971), B 266 (Ministry and existence), B 274 (Celibate existence today), B 360 (On priestly spirituality), A 77 ("Mary and the Priestly Office"), in A 31 (*Sponsa Verbi* [*Spouse of the Word*], "Priestly Existence"), in A 64 (*Pneuma und Institution* [Spirit and insti-

Adrienne's detailed commentary on the institution of the
Office of Peter (in John 21), with its presupposition that
Peter loves the Lord "more than these" and its promise
that he will die on a cross, shows the vast distance between New Testament priesthood and Old.

This leads back finally to where this book began—the
grounding of all dogmatics and spirituality in what St.
John's Gospel teaches us about Christ's loving obedience
to the Father in the Holy Spirit. This is the presupposition of the revelation of the trinitarian mystery of God's
love and of Christ's redemption of the world, when he
makes atonement for all the disobedience of mankind. St.
Thomas Aquinas had already seen that obedience was the
center of the evangelical counsels and contains the other
two. St. Ignatius followed him in that view by showing that the form of life of those who belong to Christ
comes from the obedience of Christ himself (*Spiritual
Exercises*, nos. 101ff.). It was Adrienne who emphasized
in the strongest possible terms, following St. John, the
christological foundation of obedience and took it existentially to its farthest limits, not so much in her *Buch vom
Gehorsam* [Book of obedience] (2d ed. 1993), which is intended for all Christians, as in the work that cost her spiritual blood: *Bereitschaft. Dimensionen christlichen Gehorsams*
[Readiness: Dimensions of Christian obedience] (1975).
As far as I am concerned, the secret center of my work on
the Old Testament (*Herrlichkeit* III/2 [English translation:
The Glory of the Lord VI]) is the chapter on the frightening

---

tution], "Priesthood of the New Testament"), in A 56 (*Klarstellungen*
[*Elucidations*], "The Priest I Want").

obedience of the prophets (down "The Steps of Obedience" to the obedience of Christ).[28] The question interested me not only in theology and general spirituality[29] but also in a practical way with regard to obedience in secular institutes.[30] The question must be resolved without theological or practical compromises. How can a layman working responsibly in his profession, or a priest who is obedient to his bishop, fulfill the evangelical counsel of obedience within a secular institute?

With this question, we can conclude the survey of what I have tried to do theologically since I first met Adrienne,[31] because it leads directly to the threshold of the

[28] While I confined myself to the prophets of the prophetic books, Adrienne von Speyr chose the prophet *Elijah* for her richly differentiated analysis of obedience (dictated 1950, published 1972).

[29] Cf. *Bibliographie* B 214 (Theses on the problem of authority in the Church), B 224 (The Church under the authority of Christ), B 220 (Christology and obedience in the Church), B 291 (Obedience in the Church), B 340 (Obedience in the light of the Gospel).

[30] Cf. the already mentioned lecture in Rome, (On obedience in secular institutes [*Bibliographie* B 253]).

[31] A footnote on the Johannes Verlag [St. John's Press], which was founded in 1947 first of all to publish the works of Adrienne von Speyr. Einsiedeln was chosen because of the imprimatur. Before this, two volumes had been printed in a private edition by Stocker of Lucerne (1945). In 1948 my little book *Der Laie und der Ordensstand* [The layman and the religious state] was added, together with Adrienne's translation of *The Story of a Soul* of St. Thérèse of Lisieux. From 1950 onward we tried to broaden the program by collecting writings which fitted in harmoniously with our theological and spiritual thinking (in the series *Christ heute* [The Christian today] for contemporary issues, then in the *Sigillum* series and later in the *Christliche Meister* [Christian masters] series for great texts from the Tradition). Many, if not most, of the authors we recruited were our friends or were got for us by our friends (Bernanos by Béguin). Johannes Verlag, which is continuing to

chief task we had to accomplish together, and which must now be considered: the construction and extension of the Community of St. John.

_____

expand, has not deviated from these lines right up to the present day. It tries to awaken and deepen a sense of the universality and Catholicity of Christianity. It does this by presenting, for today's readers, what is valuable and accessible in the vast Tradition of the Church (this often involves abridgments and anthologies of translated extracts) and by publishing contemporary writers who are spiritually close to us. Naturally, in the process, many different voices join in the chorus. Not everything pays off. Much that is out of print could or should not be reissued. Still, this colorful mixed orchestra has been able, time and again, to play a unified symphony. The aims of our company are clearly recognized by many people and duly appreciated.

II

PLAN:
THE COMMUNITY
OF SAINT JOHN

A. DIRECTIVES FOR ALL

1. Introduction

(1) The Community of St. John is partly already in existence, partly still under construction. It has three distinct branches—one for priests, and two for lay people, women and men. What is offered here is not the particular rule of any one of the branches but what applies in general to all three, especially with regard to the spiritual life. Some of this can be deduced from the hints given above. Nevertheless, there is much that now needs to be explained in greater detail concerning the form, spirit, and significance of the community in the present situation of the world and the Church. For more detailed information about admission and formation in internal and external life, the rules applying to the individual branches should be consulted. They are not set out here. [Shortly before his death, Fr. von Balthasar made a final revision of the present text for the definitive rules of the whole Community and the special instructions for the three branches —ED.]

Although much of the community has already been established, what follows is called a "plan". It is based on the orders received by Adrienne von Speyr, on our joint labors, and also on what can be deduced from all this about the final form the community should take. In years to come, many things will be added. Nothing is said here, for example, about the manner of election and the duration of office or about the possible dismissal of superiors. Certain points will need to be reformulated.

However, a form can be perceived, a spirit is expressed, in what follows. There can be no deviation from this form and spirit without betrayal of the primary source. The core of what stands here serves as a testament.

(2) The Church today is being persecuted or harshly criticized from within and without. More than anything else, she needs interior renewal. That is obvious to every Catholic who cares about the credibility of his Church. It is also obvious to any impartial observer that in the Church there is a great number of astonishingly positive movements of reform. Despite their individual characteristics, they all have something in common: their chief goal is not to criticize the Church in her earthly form—her shortcomings are always evident—but to come to her aid and serve her through simple, positive commitment. The last generation, in its eagerness for renewal, took up a predominantly critical stance—these were the years when we were deafened by the slogans of "progressivism" and "traditionalism". These people still occupy quite a few chairs of theology and many official positions; they also write a good deal for the newspapers. By contrast, the generation that succeeded them is looking beyond the factions toward the centrality and permanence of the faith, to give direction to their lives now threatened by the new paganism that surrounds them. Many of the old, well-established religious orders wanted to modernize themselves at any price. Still, somewhat nervously, they agonize about their spiritual identity, which makes their credibility seem, as it were, suspended. By contrast, the new impulses—some are open movements, others are

structured institutes—are distinguished by their unprob-
lematic attitude to the Church. They recognize her as the
protectress of what they seek—the authentic revelation
of God in Jesus Christ. The names of these movements
are well known and do not need to be spelled out. The
most important of them should come together in con-
gresses, so that people can meet and get to know one another, laying aside mutual prejudices and acknowledging
that basically they belong together. This would be a most
welcome initiative.

(3) Much hope for the Church of tomorrow depends
on the vitality of these movements and institutes. However, despite all their positive qualities, we must insist
on asking this question: Are they deeply enough rooted
in the mysteries of the Catholic faith to bear living witness to the unity and interconnectedness of the mysteries?
Can they give practical expression to that unity? To be
understood and lived in depth, each mystery of the faith
needs all the others. Any program for an inclusively Catholic and apostolic life should surely be constructed out
of the wholeness of the Creed, which none of us wants
to abandon. Incorporated into such a program would be
all the things the various excellent movements inscribe
on their banners as their special watchwords. Everything
then would be given its proper place. There is an obvious
objection: How can Christian fullness ever be translated
into a practical ideal by which to live? According to St.
Paul, is not the specialization of the members necessary
precisely so they can together give expression, by their
inward interdependence, to the fullness of the "Mystical

Body of Christ"? That is true. No one—and the Community of St. John is no exception—would claim to embody this fullness adequately in itself. Perhaps, though, it is worth bearing this in mind: in divine revelation there is something central, and it must be acknowledged as such; but at the same time it forms a fabric of deeply interwoven truths. These truths indwell one another to such an extent that none must be allowed to be displaced by the others.

(4) Let us be more specific. It is, of course, Jesus Christ who is the center of our faith, but only the Christ who is the Father's Son, endowed with the fullness of the Spirit, the Christ to whom the Bible bears witness. No Christology without the doctrine of the Trinity (and, of course, vice versa). And no Christology without the fulfillment of the Old Testament tradition and the missionary opening up of the Church to the whole world, the world in principle reconciled with God. It is only because this Christ is truly the Son of the Father that he can also be the "Lamb of God who takes away the sin of the world". The doctrine of redemption presupposes Christology, which in turn implies the Trinity of God. This is exactly how the Nicene Creed, based as it is on the New Testament, presents our faith to us: "For us men and for our salvation he came down from heaven". But that is not all. This doctrine of salvation, which speaks of Christ "assuming what is ours", contains within it the doctrine of the Eucharist, for in the Eucharist he gives us what is his, himself, in place of what he has taken from us. By analogy, this happens in the other sacraments celebrated

by the Church. The Son accomplished the work of our redemption through an unfailing obedience of humility and love, which went as far as the Godforsakenness of the Cross. It is inconceivable, therefore, that he would give himself to the Church without imparting to her his own attitude, both trinitarian and incarnate, to be the source of his members' unity in him and with one another. The greatest wish expressed by Christ in his prayer to the Father is "that they may all be one, even as thou, Father, art in me, and I in thee". How can that be made a reality unless the Church contains within herself a principle of unity—a principle of unity which from the beginning assents with Christ to all that the Father wills (the "Handmaid of the Lord"), a principle of unity which, by Christ's will, maintains in discipleship the disintegrating multitude of sinners (the "Rock" on whom he chooses to build his Church)? Finally, how can all this hold together in a single form which not only encompasses the fundamental statements of trinitarian and soteriological faith but also links the two basic poles of the Church as she exists in Christ—Mary and Peter?

Our community is named after the Beloved Disciple, not especially for his own sake, but because in his life and work he displays this unified vision, this holding together. We must first of all, then, say something about him as our community's *Realsymbol*, embodying its ideal and spirit.

2. The Name of the Community

(5) From the band of his disciples, the Son singled out one whom he loved in a special way, a man whose writings prove that he too—as, so to speak, the archetypal "Society of Jesus"—loved his Master in a special way. John, the profoundest interpreter of the mystery of Christ, was called by the early Church *the* theologian. It was to him that Jesus, at the climax of his redemptive work on the Cross, entrusted his Mother as a true testament, so that the two of them, Mary and John, might form the first living cell of his Church.

(6) In his Gospel, St. John, through long and deep contemplation, acknowledges Jesus to be the Logos of God. In his epistles he points entirely away from himself toward Christ. Finally, in the Apocalypse, in the vision of the Lamb of God, Old and New Testaments are united, and the whole drama of salvation is summed up. According to John:

Jesus is the one who, out of love "to the end" (13:1), is obedient (6:38; 4:34) to the Father, whose love he reveals (3:16) in the Spirit, whom he possesses "without measure" (3:34);

Mary is the one who is virginal for the sake of the Son (1:13), the intercessor who obtains by relinquishing (2:11; 1 Jn 5:15), the one who stands by the Cross in com-passion and there becomes the "Bride", the fruitful, child-bearing Church (Rev 12, where her motherhood is a bridge between the Old Testament community of faith in its Messianic birth pangs and Mother Church 12:17).

Peter is the one destined from the beginning (1:42) to be the "Rock" of the Church, the man to whom the primacy (20:15) is committed, to whom, indeed, the "greater love" is bequeathed (21:15), so that in him the unity Christ established between office and love can survive unto death (21:19), even though the Lord reserves to himself the oversight of Johannine love remaining in the world (21:22).

Our community in all its branches must try to learn from St. John the loving contemplation of the depths of God's Word. This loving contemplation takes place in personal prayer, which, through attentive listening to the Lord, attains increasingly Catholic proportions and is the prerequisite for all fruitful apostolic activity. But it also takes place in the work—of priests in their teaching and preaching, but also of the laity—of helping to defend and develop a theology which is Catholic (trinitarian) in an all-inclusive sense (for this, see B 3 and 4).

(7) John takes Mary, the "immaculate Church" (Eph 5:27), "to his own" (Jn 19:27): into the living environment of the visible Church of Peter and the other apostles. Through being made son of Mary by the Crucified Lord, John is given a special closeness to Christ's eucharistic sacrifice of his life.

The Mary-John community, established in the Petrine Church, has its origin in the Cross: from the Cross it flows, and to the Cross it returns. The way into the community is the obedience of the Cross and the poverty of the Cross. It is also a virginal community. This threefold renunciation lies henceforth at the heart of the Church as a secret seed, giving life and healing the wounds of Church and world by taking them back to the source of all salvation and healing.[1]

The Mary-John community unites and at the same time distinguishes the three branches of the Community of St. John. The Beloved Disciple has, first of all, the function of uniting Mary with Peter. As a priest, in his closeness to the Lord (he rests on his breast, 13:23; 21:20, and solemnly bears witness to the piercing of his side, 19:34–37; Rev 1:7), and in his renunciation and withdrawal (Rev 20:5 and 3:30) he performs a foundational service for the Church.

But he is also simply the man to whom, in his virginity, *the* Woman is entrusted (2:4; 19:26; cf. Eph 5). It is the Lord's will, too, that he "remains" simply in the world (21:21f.), beyond the sphere of the priestly office. The laymen's branch embodies this aspect by the work they do in the world, though always in deepest union with Mary, thus healing the fissures and wounds in the unity of the Petrine Church.

The women's branch highlights still more the Marian side of ecclesial availability. However, if this is to be Cath-

---

[1] Adrienne von Speyr was a medical practitioner. And yet in her office she had to care for souls almost more than for bodies, since patients very often wanted to discuss their personal problems under the pretext of physical illness. After her conversion, she frequently worked miraculous physical cures, but even on earth it was manifestly the special grace of spiritual healing that was given, and for her life in heaven this charism was expressly promised. She said that the community would receive a share in this gift and that its individual members would also have a part to play in this work. Those who teach, for example, would be able to heal the wounds inflicted by unbelief and error, to show the right path to doubters, and so on.

olic, it cannot be lived out self-sufficiently but only in a fruitful, ordered relationship to the male priestly side.

All three branches are expressly sent out by Christ and his Church into the world. The priests are sent not only to the People of God but into all the world (Mt 28:20), to all "the scattered children of God" (Jn 11:52). The two lay branches do not separate God's call to obedience in the Church from their secular profession (nos. 20ff. below), which only becomes "apostolic" in the full sense when united to obedience. In their secular profession, like John, they carry the "light" of Christ into the "darkness" and can heal and reconcile to the true Logos a secularized mentality. In this way all three branches point to one another and need one another. Even when the work they can do together is limited, they form an organic whole.

(8) John, with whom Mary lives and who with Peter represents the Church, does not draw attention to himself but "disappears" behind the persons he unites. He does not understand his theology in an exclusive way, either, but leaves room for the whole of the New Testament and the whole of Tradition. In the same way, too, our community would never want to take its bearings exclusively from St. John. No, with him it points to the catholicity of theological truth as the Spirit has unfolded it through the centuries of the Church. But in the disposition of the Beloved Disciple, it consecrates itself in a special way to Mary, the archetype of Holy Church, and its members regard the successor of St. Peter "as their highest superior, whose instructions they submit to by reason of their sacred bond of obedience" (CIC 590).

3. How the Community Understands
Itself as a Secular Institute

(9) The new Code of Canon Law has given secular institutes,[2] for the laity as well as for priests, a new place in the structure of the Church, juridically new but also theologically new. They are one of the two forms of life consecrated by the profession of the evangelical counsels (*instituta vitæ consecratæ*, CIC 573–746), the other being the religious state (*instituta religiosa*). It is significant that before dealing with each of these two forms separately, the Code first lays down "Norms Common to All Institutes of Consecrated Life". Secular institutes, in which consecrated lay people remain lay and the priests formally committed to the evangelical counsels do not become religious, are therefore placed on the same theological level as the religious institutes.

(10) The enhanced status of secular institutes gives us the opportunity to reflect more deeply on their theological foundation, while avoiding every kind of rash and ill-considered justification of their "secularity". It thus enables us to ask how far a Christian, who knows he has been called to follow the Lord in a special way, must "die" to the world, so that he can be sent back into it by the Lord with the message of the Kingdom.

(11) God the Father created this world and us men within it, so that, by our mutual love and care and by working

[2] Even if the community were not permanently to retain this ecclesial denomination (cf. no. 61), nothing in its theological orientation would be altered.

responsibly together in his *creation*, we may praise him, the Father. This first theme has not been abolished by the sin of man. The Creator, foreseeing what was to happen within it, found it "very good". Even "before the foundation of the world", God planned his whole work of creation in "foreknowledge of the precious blood of Christ, as of a lamb unspotted and undefiled" (1 Pet 1:19). This Son of his he sent to us, to share our secular work for thirty years, but then also, as God's conclusive Word to the world, to reveal God's triune love by his life, death, and Resurrection. Finally, by going to the Cross for our guilt and in our place, he crowned the Father's work by *reconciling* the world with God. The Father and the Son have bestowed upon us their common Spirit of love, the Spirit of *sanctification and mission*, to enable us to cooperate in bringing the world to its fulfillment in God. We do this within the world, as followers and in the attitude of the risen Lord, who lives forever in his Church. The Spirit of the Father and the Son, of the Creator and the Redeemer, urges the world on from within toward its healing and fulfillment (Rom 8:26), and at the same time he is given to those chosen and sent by the Lord (Jn 20:21f.), thus proving that the center of all the Church's secular institutes is theological and trinitarian. The Holy Spirit is both the Spirit of childhood in relation to God and the Spirit of maturity in relation to the world, the Spirit of simplicity and joy (in the midst of "persecutions", Mk 10:30) and the Spirit of prudence and perseverance, the Spirit of prayer and the Spirit of work, and finally, as has been said already (no. 7), he is the Spirit of both religious vocation and secular profession.

(12) From the faith of the Church, as well as from the particular position and function we have within her, we constantly gather new proofs of the triune love which has drawn the world into its eternal exchange and wants to draw it in ever more deeply. For this it needs the world's responsive love, and especially the love of Christians, who know that God let his Son die, like a grain of wheat in creation's field, in order to raise him up again together with all who want to follow him and transfer them into his Kingdom (Col 1:13). The beginning of this following of Christ is baptism (Rom 6) and participation in the other sacraments of the Church. However, just as Jesus on earth chose men and women to follow him more closely, leading—in the case of Mary, John, and the holy women —to the Cross, so "by the special call of God" (CIC 574, 2), this "closer following" (573, 1) of Christ in his mission in the world (574, 2) continues throughout history. The "unlimited love of God" expresses itself in the form of life of the evangelical counsels. These, "based on the teaching and example of Christ the Master, are a divine gift, which the Church has received from the Lord and ever preserves through his grace" (575).

(13) We see the evangelical counsels, chosen as "a stable form of living" (573, 1), as nothing other than the most effective way of letting go of ourselves in love, of surrendering ourselves to the service of the triune God's plan of redemption. They are the expression of the attempt we make to surrender ourselves, but they are also the ever timely reminder to persevere in that self-surrender and make it pure. They are not an end in themselves but a

training for the task that God is asking of us and entrusts to us as a grace. Even when that task is carried out entirely in the world, it can never be separated from the love that the world owes God, the love that it can only possess when it acknowledges God and shares in his love, loving God for himself and everything else for his sake. Both hope for our final happiness in God and fear of losing him are part of our creatureliness. We get beyond them when we offer ourselves up to God's infinite generosity: the generosity of his inner trinitarian life, the generosity that is displayed to us and to the world.

God deserves more love than the world gives him. Men, too, need more love than they receive from the world. Our community wants to take her place where these two needs meet.

No sinful human person can respond worthily to God's love, so the response that we try to give should consist in an ever more unreserved readiness to do God's will, of which Mary's Yes is the perfect example, so that all that God has given us, a gift beyond our measuring, we in turn may pass on to our fellow men, with unstinting generosity and in a manner appropriate to the times.

It is God who sends us in Christ to our fellow men and lets us cooperate in the building up of his Kingdom in the world. So long as we live out this mission, we do not stray from God but continue our journey toward him, even when the way leads through seeming estrangement, pain, and darkness.

(14) The fundamental and essential rule for all secular institutes applies to the members of all three branches: the

motivation for a genuine life of following Christ must come to them not only from the gospel and the Church but equally from the poverty and ignorance of the world ("*veluti ex sæculo*": *Primo feliciter*, AAS 1948, no. 2; CIC 713, 2). It is the world which convinces them time and again of the need for a radical Christian commitment. But this commitment is not just a matter of human effort. It is supported by the interior apostolic dimension of life in the counsels.

4. *Understanding the Life of the Counsels*

(15) The one goal of the three evangelical counsels, "based on the teaching and example of Christ" (CIC 575), is total self-dispossession "out of love for God" (710, 573, 1) in the service of God's Kingdom as Christ wants to bring it into this world. Attached to neither personal possessions nor the fruitfulness of marriage, the person called by God places his whole soul at God's disposal, just as the Son held himself in readiness for the Father's will. It is in this obedient readiness that the other two counsels find their complete meaning (St. Thomas Aquinas, *Summa Theologiæ* 2a–2æ 186, 8). The fact that the counsels are chosen in a "sacred bond" as a definitive form of life "does not hinder freedom, as the example of God and the blessed in heaven shows" (ibid., 88, 4, ad 1 and 3), even if the life of the counsels demands renunciations and leads, as Jesus promised, to the way of the Cross.

(16) Such dispossession enables a person to be transparent to God, to the Church, to the instructions of the

rule and to his superiors, to fellow members of the community, basically, in fact, to all men. The prudence the Christian is meant to show in his professional work is not to be separated from this call to transparency, especially transparency to God, before whose gaze the depths of the soul are laid bare. The test of whether someone is putting this into practice is his transparency to his superiors, to whom he gives an account of his conscience, but also his openness to other people, especially the members of the community. A community willed expressly by God is not a product of chance, formed of individuals thrown together at random, each pursuing his work and interests in the world. No, it is an ecclesial community with a coherent spirit bestowed from above, to which each individually and all together open themselves in gratitude, so as to order their lives in accordance with it.[3] Naturally, discussions about secular and religious matters can and should take place among them, but these have meaning and are of benefit only when they occur within the common spiritual framework of the charism bestowed and do not in any way break out of that framework.

(17) Given what has been said under number 3, there can be no problematic tensions between a genuine involvement in the world and a genuine adherence to Christ. One can reject, therefore, any watering down of the counsels —for example, for the sake of a more credible "worldliness", as will be shown below.

[3] "In our community each person should try, by the way he lives, to show as clearly as possible the spirit of the community, not by outward display like a horse on parade, but by bringing other people as much as possible into the community's spirit" (T 1862).

(18) In imparting the counsels, the Lord is calling people explicitly to follow him to the Cross. This happens more often in what is unsought than in what is voluntarily undertaken, in the spiritual more than in the physical: it means failure, contempt, mockery, calumny, and apparent abandonment by God, the things Jesus presented in his Beatitudes and endured himself in his Passion, the things St. Paul describes as the lot of an apostle (1 Cor 4:9–13). What the natural man finds obnoxious and painful, the follower of the Lord, out of love for him, should at least try to love, and if this love is not yet or no longer perceptible, it should nevertheless govern the innermost ground of his will. Because he loves the Lord, he is really glad that, despite his unworthiness, the Lord takes him seriously and makes use of him for purposes known only to him.

(19) Even when it invites us daily to take up our cross, the gospel is Good News. If you live by the gospel, you must radiate joy: the joy of being a Christian and being allowed to live in the light of God's grace. This is the joy of being called to a closer following of the Lord in order to be more available for work for the Kingdom; it brings with it much "tribulation and distress" (Rom 8:35), but it also allows us to cast all our cares upon God. This is the joy of being able to share in the Beatitudes of Jesus (including the final ones). Joyful harmony must reign between Christian freedom and the practice of obedience (to Church and profession).

5. The Spirit of Obedience

(20) Obedience in the community should envelop the entire existence of the member. In the case of the lay members, this applies not only to their interior life but also to their secular profession. The personal responsibility, initiative, and creative freedom with which they practice their profession stand beneath the blessing of ecclesial obedience: in obedience they are accepted, and in obedience they are put to use. A person's profession is not a private sphere altogether remote from obedience. "Everyone who enters must realize that the call of the Lord is more important than the call of one's profession."[4] Members should therefore be led back spiritually to the point at which they are ready for everything.

(21) When someone enters so young that his professional training still lies ahead of him, he will discuss his professional plans, as well as his aptitudes and inclinations, with his superior or superiors, who, after hearing all that has been presented and after discussion with the council (no. 93), will consider the matter in prayer and make the final decision. When the candidate is insufficiently certain about the state of life he should choose, before being admitted he should be sent off for some serious spiritual exercises, and for some time afterward he should be spiritually accompanied in his daily life.

(22) Cases where a decision needs to be made between a vocation to the priesthood and vocation to the life of

---

[4] N XI, 415.

the counsels in a secular profession must be further clarified by even longer exercises. The instructions of St. Ignatius in his *Spiritual Exercises* (no. 15) are to be followed. Candidates who are already on the path to priesthood, or who have completed it, should be examined by means of spiritual exercises that introduce the life of the counsels, in order to test their suitability for the Community of St. John. Where such exercises reveal that a seminarian would be better suited to the life of the counsels in a secular profession rather than a sacred one, this should be discussed with the bishop or his representative.

(23) Even someone who enters having completed his training for a secular profession, or is already practicing it, should likewise be led, in the exercises, to total detachment. Having taken account of the candidate's general disposition, and after discussion with his council (no. 93), the superior must decide whether or not he is right for his chosen profession. The candidate should be aware that the disciple called by the Lord leaves behind everything, so that he can be ready for any undertaking. He will also recall that the disciples in the Gospel, at Jesus' bidding, left everything behind and followed him as someone commissioned by God, even before they had recognized that he was himself God. It goes without saying that the instruction given by the superior to take up or continue a course of study for a particular profession obliges the superior himself and his successors to abide by the consequences of that momentous command and not to alter it without grave reasons. On the other hand, where the reasons are a member's failure in one post or his urgently

being needed for another, the superior should, wherever possible, confer with his assembled council, so that the member in question may understand and approve the reasons that are decisive for the member himself or for the community.

(24) Nevertheless, everyone should be aware that true obedience involves complying with the superior's order even when he does not understand it or not completely; the example of Jesus and Mary should convince him of that.

(25) Throughout his public life, Jesus was accompanied by the Father and was conscious of his love, even when something difficult was demanded of him. But, at the beginning of the Passion, the moment came when the Father had to conceal his love from the Son behind what seemed like sheer duty and naked demand. This was so that the Son, for the world's redemption, could yield the whole of his will, which humanly at first shrank back, to the unconditional task. The Father acted in this way, not out of arbitrariness or cruelty, but in accordance with the Trinity's salvific decree. The follower of Christ may likewise, when God so decrees, come to experience something of the hardness of the Passion's obedience, and he should prepare himself for such a possibility by contemplative prayer.

(26) This basic principle applies to priests as well. Their obedience to the bishop is perfectly compatible with the obedience demanded in the community—as many communities of priests show.

(27) Since obedience is based on a fundamental openness and readiness to receive, the New Testament constantly emphasizes that the Christian must be ready for "mutual, fraternal admonition" (Rom 12:10; Gal 5:13; 6:1f.; Eph 5:21; Phil 2:1f.). It also stresses how much this admonition needs to be practiced in love and humility. In connection with fraternal admonition, opportunity must be given for harmonizing in open dialogue, as far as possible, divergent standpoints on important matters of Church doctrine and practice. Each should listen to the arguments of the other; each should be able to tell the other how he is causing offense or encountering misunderstanding.

(28) Only someone who is tried and tested in obedience can undertake the office of superior. Such a person will realize that the authority he has to demand things of people requires of him no less obedience to the gospel, to the rules of the community, and ultimately, in every specific case, to God himself than is required of his subordinates, who obey for the sake of Christ. In the community the office of superior must never be interpreted or exercised as a merely administrative or subsidiary function.

(29) The hardness of the Father's demands in Gethsemane presupposes that he accompanied the Son's whole life and prayer with perceptible fatherly love. Similarly, the superior has the strict obligation to accompany, with fatherly love and care, those under him. He can do this only if he lives in constant prayerful intimacy with God and so can pass on to those entrusted to him, not his own possibly arbitrary decisions, but that which is truly the will of God.

(30) Mutual trust between leaders and the led, promoted by open discussion, together with unanimity in the spirit of the community, will enable us, at decisive moments, to rise above our own points of view (cf. Acts 21). Nevertheless, the person who obeys does not have the right to adjust his obedience to the degree of perfection that he imagines the superior has attained.

(31) Every member accepts his mission, whatever his profession, with a full measure of personal responsibility and initiative. The individual can entrust the free management of work beyond his powers to the sure guidance of the Holy Spirit, and he should not hesitate to take up difficult and exposed posts, where he stands more or less alone. The fact that other people, like-minded people, within the community are giving him inner strength for his task does not need to be admitted to his associates. Only *one* connection should be visible to all: the connection with God and the Church.

(32) Even a person working independently should allow himself to be directed and, if necessary, advised about everything relevant to his interior life. It will be sensible, therefore, if, in a given professional sphere, a qualified member is chosen by his colleagues to act as advisor. This person will assist the superior and relieve him of the responsibility of giving advice on specialized subjects beyond his professional competence. The special advisors should not as a rule be needed for resolving interior conflicts of a religious or ethical kind for which the confes-

sor is qualified or which can also be discussed with the superior.

(33) The members are not to discuss the deficiencies of third parties among themselves. On the other hand, it is their duty to draw to the superior's attention the more serious faults that they notice. For the informant, once this has been done, the matter is settled; responsibility falls upon the superior to take the precautionary measures needed. Everyone should regard this duty to inform as an expression of Christian love within the organism of Christ's Mystical Body. Moreover, even in old age, everyone should be grateful for the reprimand that helps him on the way of Christ.

6. *The Spirit of Virginity*

(34) Those called to virginity are privileged to be drawn into the direct relationship of Christ and his Church (to which, as to its model, marriage is oriented, Eph 5). This special grace is bestowed by the Lord (Mt 19:12) for the sake of a "greater fruitfulness" (CIC 599) in the Kingdom of God. Trusting not in their own powers but in God's strengthening grace, they thankfully and joyfully embrace this form of life.

The period of initiation into the community, especially the exercises in preparation for it, presents an opportunity for turning oneself, with the help of grace, toward the vow of virginity and for turning away from earlier faults.

(35) The fruitfulness of the virginal person is not something purely spiritual, but, like the fruitfulness of poverty and obedience, it is bound up with the Incarnation. We can see this in the eucharistic fruitfulness of the body of Jesus, whose total self-giving brings forth his Bride (Eph 5:27) and constantly generates new life from her. "The body is for the Lord, and the Lord for the body", and so, as a consequence, the body will be raised up with the Lord's (1 Cor 6:13f.). The virginal person, of either sex, is drawn in a special way into the marriage of Christ and his Church. This is a marriage of male and female, but it remains virginal and excludes all the disturbances of a purely earthly sexuality. The mother/son relationship of Mary and John reminds us of its true nature.

(36) Those who live virginally do not complain about the loneliness connected with this renunciation, and they do not try to obtain a substitute, inside or outside the community, in more or less sensually colored friendships, or even in purely worldly ones; nor do they try artificially to imprint upon the community the character of a "family business". Instead, in the spirit of the Lord, his Mother, and the saints, they give to "all men, and especially to those who are of the household of the faith" (Gal 6:10), their genuinely human sympathy and love. When celibacy is lived unreservedly in imitation of Christ, with his attitude, as a share in his Cross, it gives man, whether priest or layman, a fatherhood that cannot be explained in naturalistic terms, and on a woman it bestows a motherhood. Both of these mysteries have their source in the Son's taking of a body and in the virginal Motherhood of Mary.

(37) "Nowadays the remedy of keeping one's distance, of not wanting to see [things to do with the body], has lost its force."[5] It is now a question of passing beyond the erotic in an intelligent and calmly reflective way. In everything to do with the body, we need simplicity.[6] However, this does not make caution superfluous. Members avoid, therefore, all unnecessary displays of affection, except by way of welcome and farewell, or if their profession demands the physical care of their fellow men.[7]

7. The Spirit of Poverty

(38) Evangelical poverty in secular institutes can be practiced in various ways. In some of them, the members will manage their income themselves, though they will submit accounts of it and accept, without objection, instructions aimed at genuine poverty. In others, at least from the time of final vows or promises, everything will be deposited in a common account, from which individuals receive what they need for the expenses appropriate to their situation. Since financial questions are settled in the different branches of the Community of St. John, they fall under the more detailed rules and will not be discussed here. Let it be sufficient to point out that the foundress gave the women's branch the instruction that all earnings not absolutely required for the immediate future should be anonymously donated at short intervals, say half-yearly, to needy persons or to Church charities. In no circum-

[5] T 1703.
[6] T 1646.
[7] T 1709, 1712.

stances may the community hoard goods for itself or use them for purposes serving its own prosperity and prestige; it should, so far as this is possible today, follow the words of the Sermon on the Mount.

(39) Poverty is above all a thing of the spirit, of the will, and also of penance. This is to be taken especially to heart in secular institutes, where many members may earn a great deal of money and acquire things taken for granted in their professional milieu—large collections of books, travel, means of transport, various kinds of entertainment, use of the mass media, etc. For someone vowed to Christian poverty, these things may by no means be taken for granted. The community must be stricter even than many religious orders in the care it takes to ensure that, even in the midst of surrounding prosperity, real poverty is practiced and sometimes even acutely felt. This demands not only persistent vigilance on the part of superiors but equally persistent self-examination by each individual to determine the minimum that is absolutely necessary for his Christian task in the world.

(40) Every member of the community, who has vowed poverty, must remind himself that none of the things he uses for doing his work belongs to him. That applies not only to accommodation, food, clothing, transport, and so on, but also to all the spiritual, cultural, professional, and other achievements he may have acquired. Gifts, St. Paul teaches, are bestowed on individuals for the benefit of the community; it is not the individual who decides how he is to be used but the Church.

(41) The possession of anything, whether material or spiritual, is a form of power, which, though not necessarily evil in itself, is still the most seductive thing in the world —and in the Church. The tactic of first securing a position of power so you can then go on (allegedly) to spread the gospel fails to make the necessary discernment of spirits; the history of the Church's missions provides examples of this. No one was more publicly and profoundly humbled by the Lord than Peter, who was to receive the highest office; no one was more painfully drawn into the nakedness of the Cross than John, to say nothing of Mary. Following our Lord's own example, the "greatest" among you must be the servant of all. Again and again, communities have foundered at this point. Even when individuals are poor, if the monastery or congregation is rich, the disaster has usually already happened. This is the greatest danger for secular institutes, especially the culturally influential ones. It can be avoided only if the institutes maintain unceasing vigilance and take seriously the Lord's admonition and example.

8. The Spirit of Penance and Joy

(42) In most of the professions taken up by members and seriously lived out by them in the spirit of the community, there are many different opportunities for thinking about penance and for actually doing it. Penances imposed by one's mission, especially when they are humbling and accepted in the Spirit of Christ, are often more blessed than self-chosen penitential exercises.

(43) This does not prevent each person asking himself whether, in following our Lord, he is doing enough penance: for his own sins, for the failings of those entrusted to him, and for the needs of the Church in the world, in whose great collective guilt he shares. He should discuss with his confessor the penances he wants to take upon himself. He should also ask his confessor for some penances he has not chosen himself, for which he should render an account. Acts of penance should be discreet and carried out, as far as possible, without other people knowing.

(44) The superior has the duty to reprimand those subject to him and the right to impose punishments. For publicly given scandal he can demand a public acknowledgement of guilt, which is to be made with a thankful heart. Even if, in a particular case, the person concerned does not feel guilty, the penance imposed on him is to be willingly accepted in the knowledge that we never do enough penance for our guilt. The superior should forbid acts of penance that seem exaggerated or dangerous to health.

(45) According to our Lord's command, penance must not block the shining of Christian joy (cf. Mt 6:16f.). Joy, as already noted, is inseparable from a life for the sake of the Good News; in fact, it is demanded by it. It should precisely be a cause of joy, again according to the Lord's command and the example of his apostles, "when men revile you and persecute you and utter all kinds of evil against you falsely on my account" (Mt 5:11f.): it is a sign

that God is taking seriously the renunciation we make in following his Son. The fact that penance can seem hard and subjectively impose on our souls the burden of interior darkness and exterior temptation is no reason for forgetting the objective joy in our decision to follow Jesus. We have the obligation to show that joy, which is the ultimate reason for all that is difficult about following him, to those who are around us and whose eyes are upon us.

9. Discretion

(46) Nothing in the structure of the Church is secret, and this is also true of the community. However, to be effective in specific situations, it must insist on great discretion in all matters. Members will not disclose their membership without good reason, but if they are seriously asked, they will not deny it either. Above all, they will not speak about other people's membership, especially those who would be hampered in their work were it known that they were members of a religious community.

(47) Discretion does not mean sectarian secretiveness. Not only the individual member but the community as a whole remains outwardly open to all the authentic concerns of the Church. It does not cut itself off from contemplative and active orders, communities, and movements that are approved by the Church but with a different constitution from its own. Wherever it is beneficial, the community will work with them, well aware that differentness in charism contributes to the completeness and richness of the Mystical Body of Christ. Other move-

ments and groups must not be judged by the standards of our own spirituality. The Church has room for much that differs from our own approach, so we must joyfully fit in and subordinate ourselves to her greater wholeness. Our community maintains contact with other communities and groups, not least with contemplative monasteries. We are always ready to learn from their way of life and to establish a two-way relationship between ourselves and those who differ from us, in so far as this is mutually beneficial.

10. Balance

(48) In all three branches, and in all the different areas of its activity, the community's form of life demands a constant effort at interior balance.

First, there is the balance between work and prayer. The person who has not lost his intimate relationship with God by neglecting prayer and does not imagine work for God is prayer enough ought constantly to feel a longing for a new intimacy with God, even if it costs him something to interrupt his work or to sacrifice profitable reading or well-earned rest in order to repair to God, our true home, our best teacher, and our abiding rest. This tilting of the balance toward God is given to us if, when we pray, we are not self-seeking and if, for the love of God, we persevere in unavoidable times of aridity. Let us cultivate in ourselves the joy and freedom of praying more than is strictly required and also take advantage, for interior recollection, of the inevitable pauses and times of waiting that come our way. Let us subdue our craving for activism, whether in our professions or in the community.

(49) At least once a year, everyone should make a retreat for a few days in order to devote himself to prayer and meditation on Sacred Scripture; those who need to should do this under the guidance of an experienced priest. During these days the balance which is absolutely essential in our kind of life and yet can be so easily threatened should be regained and deepened.

(50) When there is a sufficient number of members, an effort should be made, at least in the lay communities, to form a "contemplative core". This will consist of members concerned with the internal side of our work, or those who through age have been freed from professional employment, or those able to withdraw from it for a time to devote themselves to prayer, contemplation, the reading of Scripture, and deeper study of matters concerning divine revelation. Their chief object in doing this is not to draw new strength for themselves but by their prayer to undergird all that the community is doing and to make sacrifices for it, including, as always, the intentions of the whole Church.

(51) Those in authority should take care to see that, in the activities of the community as a whole, balance is maintained between working independently and working in groups, whether small or large. If someone has an apostolically important post, say in a non-Catholic situation, he should be withdrawn for a common enterprise only in exceptional circumstances.

(52) The professionally busy person must not make himself mentally remote from the community. He should not expend all his powers of creativity and love outside the community and then lead a merely bored and taciturn existence within. He has a definite responsibility for his brothers and sisters in the community; he owes them his example, help, and cooperation. This does not mean that he should indiscreetly interfere in other people's affairs. The atmosphere emanating from the community —"love, joy, peace, patience, kindness, goodness, faithfulness, gentleness, self-control" (Gal 5:22)—should, through each member, influence those around us and be an example to them, just as the Church as a whole must be a light shining for all (Mt 5:14f.) and a constant example of love (Jn 17:22).

(53) For the sake of balance, even a person working independently should allow himself to be guided in all aspects of his external life, and he should listen to what he is told about his conduct, his demeanor, and the impression he makes on other people. Being a child in the Gospel sense is something no one can afford to forget.

11. New Life, New Departures

(54) Everyone should be aware of the fact that spiritual immobility is the death of life in the counsels—for individuals and, in the long run, for every community in the Church as well.

This means that, trusting in God, we must begin anew each day with ourselves and with other people. Persuading ourselves that strain in our relationship with God or with another human being is inevitable and unalterable, or dressing up such faults with the fashionable words of psychology, is an offense against faith, hope, and charity, as well as against self-discipline and mortification. God is unceasingly ready to help us with his grace to start afresh, and Jesus, who is our way, is unfailingly on hand with new and different beginnings. Only if our own spirits are being "renewed every day" (2 Cor 4:16) can the spirit of the community remain young.

This means that each member must make sure he does not become blasé about the demands of life in the counsels; on the contrary, he must take up his cross daily as something new, each time in the spirit in which he made his original decision about this kind of life. God is ever new, and so, looking to him, we should be perpetually "renewed" (Col 3:10).

12. Old Age, Sickness, and Death

(55) Special attention is to be devoted to aging members. They must not be allowed to feel "redundant" and neglected, because then bitterness and resignation will set in. When special facilities are granted them, they should bear in mind that, especially by their prayer, they make a valuable contribution to the whole community, which everyone acknowledges. The spirit of the counsels and of joy should remain alive in them to the very end.

(56) In sickness one should be content and not appear hard to please, while the healthy should, as far as possi-

ble, lovingly take care of the sick. They are not to be left on their own either at home or in hospital, and during visits every effort should be made unobtrusively to raise up their spirits. The sick person, however, should see his condition, like everything else God decrees for him, as a grace specially intended for him, to be accepted in grateful patience and in union with the sufferings of our Lord.

(57) Since we are all striving for eternal life, the condition of the gravely ill and dying is not to be concealed from them. This means, of course, that those who nurse and visit them must give them their special compassion and their company. If the dying man during his life has already prepared himself for eternity, he should succeed in giving an example of a Christian death to those at his bedside. All are to accompany him with their prayers to the very end.

13. The Organization and Leadership of the Community of St. John

(58) The community is international. As already mentioned, it is divided into three branches: a priests' branch and, for the laity, one for women and one for men. Apart from the generally applicable guidelines presented here, each branch has its own particular statutes concerning admission, formation, community life, and so on.

(59) Each branch has a leader responsible for everything, but the leadership of the community as a whole lies in the hands of a member of the priests' branch. For a council

he has the leaders of the individual branches as well as the representatives of important projects taken care of by the community (such as the publishing business, *Johannes Verlag*, for example). The council meets together periodically and must be consulted in all important decisions about the affairs of the community or even of individual members. In accordance with *Provida Mater* III, 4, it is desirable for each branch to have a house of its own for the purposes mentioned there.

(60) The members of the priests' branch are to be available to the lay members for care and counsel, insofar as their ministry permits it, and to see in this a duty belonging to the very essence of the community. Longer or closer collaboration between members of the men's and women's branches requires special permission.

(61) The Holy Father alone has the authority to change the status of the Community of St. John as a secular institute.

B. THE PRIESTS' BRANCH

1. "Secular Priesthood"

(62) According to the new Code of Canon Law, diocesan priests may[1] live in the evangelical counsels and yet retain their canonical status (CIC 711). The same Code assigns common guidelines to both secular institutes and religious as "institutes of consecrated life" (573–606). It would be absurd to look for the "secularity" of a priest thus consecrated in anything except his permanent "exposure"—as a pastor looking after a parish in the world, as a teacher of theology or catechism, or as a diocesan administrator. However, in this exposure, he must provide, by his active charity, help and support to his brethren, first and foremost those in the community (713, 3).

---

[1] Adrienne von Speyr would prefer to say "should". "Priesthood without the life of the counsels", she said once, "is really a concession on the part of the Church. Every priest should be in the life of the counsels. As things are now . . . both the rule and the wife are missing. For the secular priest, the parish is the focus of his vocation; apart from that, in a sense he is free. The secular clergy have almost completely dispensed themselves from poverty: Why shouldn't a secular priest be a millionaire? Celibacy means that you sacrifice having a family for the sake of the parish. The end is external. The main motive for the sacrifice is the priest's professional work: as a celibate, he has more time at his disposal. . . . Obedience to the bishop has become very meager. You say Yes or No to him, according to need. You explain things to him." Assistant priests living the life of the counsels ought to be a "leaven" in the parish. This is not always easy. "The pastor has the authority to get his assistant to conform to the life-style of the rectory", and "very soon [the assistant] will forget his special position. From this point of view, it would be advisable to take over whole parishes", and then the community could place "pastors as well as assistants" (N I/2, 284–85).

In line with what was said at the beginning about the theological place of secular institutes, the life of the counsels is not an escape from the world of creation. On the contrary, it is an expression of being sent by Christ into the world in order to transform it from within by the "leaven" of God's Kingdom. It is clear from the Gospel that this kind of mission is incompatible with an interior "conformity to this world" (Rom 12:2).

2. The Community's Image of the Priest

(63) Jesus Christ unites in himself the three principal offices of the Old Testament. He fulfills the *Prophet's* office of announcing the Word of God by being that Word in person. He is *Priest* by offering, not some external sacrifice, but himself. And he is *King* or *Shepherd* (as the peoples of antiquity called their king, who in Israel's case was supposed to pasture his people on behalf of God). As Good Shepherd, he gives up his life for his sheep (Jn 10:11, 17) in the manner of a priest, and in that very act he is also king (Jn 18:37) and supreme prophetic revelation of God's love for the world (Jn 3:16).

Since Jesus is man and therefore a man in relation to other men, from the very beginning of his ministry he gathers around himself cooperators (Mt 4:18ff.; Mk 3:13ff.; Jn 1:35–51). To them he gives, first of all, a share in his powers and then, at the time of his Passion, the plenitude of the priesthood. "Do this in memory of me", "Whose sins you forgive. . . ." Finally, the office of shepherd, as the summit of all office, is bestowed upon Peter ("son of John", Jn 21:15ff.), but only when he confesses his "greater love" (Jn 21:15) and hears the promise that he will follow Jesus to the Cross (Jn 21:18). While Old Testament priesthood has been superseded by Jesus' self-offering (Heb 9:11), the office of shepherd, conferred on Peter and the Church, has been given an entirely new character by the Cross, one which incorporates within it the unity in Christ of the three Old Testament offices. The concept of "shepherd", which was passed on to the Church from the Old Testament by Jesus, also shows that there can only be a shepherd in the full New Testament sense when an individual, sent and consecrated, takes up the task of "pasturing" a (more or less) Christian community.[2] "Pastor" means literally "one who feeds", one who provides pasture. It goes without saying that as nourishment he offers nothing except what he himself has received: our eternal food, Jesus Christ.

(64) In the light of Jesus' self-offering, the life of self-giving, in the ecclesial form of an explicit, lifelong commitment to the three evangelical counsels, can be seen as the most appropriate response on the part of a man called to pastoral office in the Church. The apostles formed a community, called together by the Lord, even though each was allocated his own field of work. Similarly, though the priests of a diocese, as the bishop's helpers, make up a presbyteral college, it would be ex-

---

[2] Courage has always been needed for this task, and today it is needed more than ever. There are known cases where individuals out of cowardice take refuge in closed communities where they feel they are protected from an exposed way of life. At the same time, we are not saying anything against genuine vocations to contemplative or active orders and congregations.

tremely advantageous to the Church's pastors if, in addition to this, despite their isolation in the world, they formed a close brotherly community (CIC 715, 1; 716, 2; 717, 3).

(65) The life of the counsels in a community of priests can be described as primarily christological, in the sense that, in its mission and grace, it seeks to imitate Jesus' own way of life. It is also, secondarily, Marian and ecclesiological (as is, in a primordial way, the life of religious and consecrated virgins), in the sense that priests, like all other believers, are members of the Church.

(66) In the universal Church, the bishop of Rome is the efficacious sign of the Church's unity. Every bishop is the same sign of unity for his local Church. By analogy, the individual priest—always as a member of the presbyteral college of the local Church—is the irreplaceable bond of unity in his parish or field of work, without prejudice to the different functions entrusted to other members of the parish or group in question. He can fulfill this role even better if he leaves all the many kinds of secondary matters to his cooperators, so that he can devote himself with more freedom to his spiritual and pastoral duties (cf. Acts 6:3f.).

On other matters, the norms common to all communities of diocesan priests in the consecrated life (CIC 573–606) apply to the Community of St. John.

3. Ecclesial Status

(67) The priests' branch of the Community of St. John sees itself as a superdiocesan community of priests, who are under the authority of their bishop (CIC 715) but at the same time, following (715, 1) the three evangelical counsels by a special consecration (712), submit themselves also to a superior in the community for the enhancement of their Christian life. They show their communion by praying for one another, by meeting together, and by personal contacts that are mutually strengthening (716). In today's world they bear witness to the undiminished vitality of the Good News and try, as far as possible, to sanctify the world from within (710).

(68) Both the meetings they hold together and their personal efforts as individuals should serve an ever better understanding of the spirit of the community, as described by the guidelines. Since this spirit is Catholic, in no way should it alienate members from the rest of their brother priests. When meetings are concerned with questions of general interest in the Church, they should be open to any of their brother priests who are interested.

4. Entry and Formation

(69) Admission to the community takes place after a retreat given in the spirit of the community, after a thorough introduction to the theological nature of the evangelical counsels and their practical implications for the priestly life, and after a full account of the candidate's previous

life has been given to the superior of the branch. Should a postulant need a more extensive introduction to the life of the counsels and the spirit of the community, the superior ought to obtain the permission of the bishop.

(70) The normal study of theology should be pursued with the requisite seriousness and zeal, remembering that the patron of the community is the *Theologos*. He will help members to see that deep knowledge of the mysteries of God is part of their vocation and that this kind of knowledge requires the permanent fruitful interaction of study, spiritual reading of Scripture and the great works of the theological and spiritual tradition, and personal meditation.

(71) All members of the priests' branch should be so acquainted with the *Spiritual Exercises* of St. Ignatius by study and personal experience that they will be in a position to give the Exercises themselves and guide the retreatant in the spirit and according to the directives in the book.

(72) Meetings begin with common meditation on and discussion of a text of Sacred Scripture. In addition to the concerns of the community, pastoral questions and important cases of conscience should be discussed. To solve these, everyone must reach the greatest possible measure of agreement.

(73) Entry should take place mainly in the younger years. However, older priests may also enter, especially if there is the hope that they will contribute something to the enhancement of the community.

5. Obligations

(74) The various obligations concerning meditation, the Breviary and other spiritual exercises, the Sacrament of Penance and the periodic opening up of conscience, the general spirit of priesthood and fraternity are laid down in the particular rules. They do not go beyond what should be expected of any zealous priest and largely cover the ground mapped out in CIC 719.

However, one additional remark should be made. The things mentioned in the rules are meant, not to make individuals feel self-satisfied, but to move them to ever new initiatives in following our Lord and Master and serving our fellow men.

6. Understanding the Evangelical Counsels

Poverty

(75) In their parishes, which contain people who are poor in the material sense, priests must give an example of evangelical poverty, especially "poverty in spirit". They do this by regarding all the advantages they have had over other people in education and perhaps in prestige as being for the service of those people, and as much as possible they have time for the needs of all. They keep an open door and an open hand. Similarly with their standard of living: the greatest simplicity in accommodation, unpretentiousness in dress and food, in cultural and technical enrichments, and in everything that may give the appearance of "clerical opulence". Vacations should be inexpensive and undemanding.

(76) Whatever individuals possess over and above their salary must be known to the superior of the community. They draw up an annual account of their use of their income and, if they have any, of their property. The bishop, when he makes his visitation, should also be allowed to inspect this account. They concern themselves with the material difficulties of the community's members and of their confreres. They pay a fixed sum into the community's bank account to cover the expenses of the meetings or subventions that they have discussed together.

When they take out insurance policies, whether obligatory or otherwise, they restrict themselves to the lowest rates.

Celibacy

(77) Priestly celibacy, in inward attitude and outward conduct, is conformed in the closest way to the Eucharist of the Lord, in which he keeps his Body ready, with all its capacities, as a gift for the Father to bestow on mankind in the holy Spirit. Our Lord's eucharistic giving of his whole Body would be unthinkable if, even in the most devout spirit of the Old Testament, he had been married. The christological motivation of the priest's renunciation of marriage gives his being and activity a fruitfulness which enables him to become "father", "mother", "wet nurse" (St. Paul) to those entrusted to him.

(78) The members of the community do not let themselves be deceived by the opinions of those who do not fully understand that the body is for the Lord and the

Lord for the body. In their relationships with women, they take as their model the nobility and naturalness of Jesus. While maintaining total simplicity in their attitude to sexuality, they look on the consecration of their sexual powers to God as a most serious matter, affecting their priestly vocation at the deepest level. Ready for a possibly lifelong struggle, they regard the unsatisfied longing for completion and the loneliness in an often unsuccessful priestly ministry as a grace of participation in the Cross of the Lord.

Obedience

(79) Christ's world-redeeming obedience begins with the act of his Incarnation (Phil 2:8), marks every action of his life (Jn 12:49), and attains its ultimate expression on the Cross. There, renouncing his intimacy with the Father (Mk 15:34), he bears all the estrangement from God of the sin of the world (Jn 1:29) and by his obedience overcomes it (Jn 16:33). Undertaken in faith and love in the following of Christ, the obedience of the priest must be resolute and radical (CIC 601). Sometimes it will not seem difficult, because the wishes or commands of authority (bishop, rule, community superior) are in line with his own inclinations. However, he needs to be prepared for possible conflict situations, in which the seriousness of dispossessing himself of his own will in the service of God's Kingdom will be only too evident. In the spirit of St. John, his obedience is a constant participation, especially in hard trials, in the unreserved readiness of Mary ("Behold the handmaid of the Lord") and the demands made on Peter ("Whither you would not", Jn 21:18).

Love and Joy

(80) The life of the counsels, as the general instructions have already said, makes sense only as an expression of our love for God and as a means of remaining faithful. Despite the many misunderstandings of outsiders, this motivation has a special significance in the life of a priest. When the life is lived rightly, the attitude of a pastor in harmony with the counsels has a direct power of persuasion.

All the priest's renunciations must be an expression of the joy of being privileged to serve Christ and mankind. Whether he is pervaded with a feeling of divine consolation or "shares abundantly in Christ's sufferings" (2 Cor 1:5), he has the joy of knowing that both experiences bear fruit for the parish—for its comforting and strengthening and for the increase of its hope (ibid., 1:6–7). He must not dwell on his own fortunes in the presence of other people. They will bring forth their fruit if he bears them with a pastor's joy.

7. *Membership*

(81) The community has a core group of full members. These, after about two years of initiation into the spirit of the community and having satisfied the probationary requirements of the superior, decide to make a temporary promise and then, after a further five years (CIC 723), make a definitive bond. The first promise is not made before ordination to the diaconate; the definitive bond is not made until after probation in priestly ministry. This

final promise is preceded by a retreat and an opening up of conscience to the superior of the community.

(82) As already mentioned in number 68, priests interested in the spiritual orientation of the community can be affiliated to this core group. Without undertaking any obligations, they can take part in certain of the meetings of the community.

8. Leaving the Community

(83) When a member has made only temporary promises, he can leave freely or, for good cause, be asked to leave by the superior (cf. CIC 720) after consultation with his council (726, 1). When the definitive promise has been made, the superior must inform the bishop of his departure (727, 1).

C. THE WOMEN'S BRANCH

1. Admission

(84) Anyone who wants to be accepted into the women's branch of the Community of St. John must have the firm will to spend her whole life in following Christ in his evangelical counsels and in engagement in the world for the good of her fellow men, the precise form of which will be decided by the community.

The age of admission extends from majority to the thirtieth year. Only exceptionally and for special reasons will older persons be admitted.

The candidate must be healthy in mind and body. Her character must be such that she will find no great difficulty in fitting into a group that has not chosen itself.

Those who have not attained the age of majority and are interested in the community should be spiritually accompanied and advised by a member of the community approved by the superior without any pressure being put on her to join.

2. Choice of Profession and Formation

(85) What was said in the general instructions about obedience in relation to the choice of secular profession and about the indifference that requires (no. 23) must be adhered to exactly. Only thus do sacred vocation and secular profession really become one; only thus is the latter placed under the blessing of the former. Young people who have already set up a definite goal for their lives

should not feel that what the community here requires for the sake of a high spiritual good is an excessive demand, especially when they remember the mobility demanded nowadays of individuals in the labor market, even within one reasonably large business. After all, Peter and his companions had to leave their secular occupation to become, as the Lord said, fishers of men, something of which they would never have dreamed.

(86) Even when postulants have begun or finished their studies or professional training, they should strive to be straightforwardly available for all the needs of the community. A retreat of suitable duration will have led them into this attitude. After serious examination of the postulant's talents, the final decision is taken by the superior of the community in consultation with his council.

(87) With the help of her council and clerical adviser, the superior decides whether and for how long a postulant should, before her secular training or professional activity, receive her first introduction to the spirit and practices of the community. This can be done within a residence of the community or by individual members. During this period care must be taken to ensure that the general spiritual orientation of the community has been properly understood and that the postulant's aptitudes have been sufficiently examined.

    If this has been ensured at the beginning, spiritual and theological formation can take place concurrently with secular activity (further studies, professional training or practice), which, for the time being, should be as limited as possible. Longer periods of vacation, as well as weeks of leave, can also be used for continuing formation (but without damaging the postulant's health).

(88) In serious cases, for example, when a member is unsuccessful in a particular job, or where there is grave moral danger, the leadership of the community can require a move to another place or, in an extreme situation, a change of profession. Needless to say, this must only be done after rigorous inquiries and after discussion with the member concerned and with the council, to which in this case the specialist adviser (cf. nos. 32, 104) belongs.

(89) On entry to the community, a detailed account must be given of the whole of the person's previous life, of her development both interior and exterior. She must also make clear her reasons for wanting to join the community. These disclosures can be given to the superior general or to a person appointed by her.

(90) During her formation, the future member must be carefully introduced to the practice of contemplative prayer. This can be done through instruction from an experienced member of the women's community or by a member of the priests' branch. Points for meditation can be given orally or in writing, and there can also be frequent discussions. A sensible daily program, which must not be overloaded, is laid down in individual cases by the rules.

(91) In addition to prayer, study, and professional activity, there should be sufficient time for learning and carrying

out housework. At the same time care must be taken to ensure that there is time for relaxation. In the periods of common recreation, everyone should have the opportunity to take part, to bring up subjects of general interest, and so practice the art of conversation. Difficult questions should also be discussed in common and in such a way that no disagreement arises and a solution as far as possible acceptable to all emerges. In form and content, recreation should be profitable to all with regard to their work.

(92) There can also be activities outside the community, for example, work in a parish or some other suitable setting.

(93) The first, temporary promises are made after two years at the earliest and, after a retreat, final promises from five to eight years later, preceded by a general confession. If a candidate at the end of the first two years has not attained the necessary maturity, the temporary promises can be postponed for a time, but no longer than a year.

3. The Life of Prayer

(94) In addition to the instructions applying to all, the following points are to be observed. Each day a specified period of time will be devoted to contemplative prayer, Mass, spiritual reading, and the Rosary or an equivalent part of the Breviary. As far as possible, Vespers will be said in common. When members are being overtaxed, the

superior can allow a lightening of this program. Certain weekends must be set aside for recollection and meditation, and each year there should be a common retreat.

4. Profession and Work

(95) The professions they practice should give each member the opportunity to cooperate, according to her capacity, in the building up of God's Kingdom in the world. This may be in academic or some other work, on her own or in a team. Each of these in its own way can be fruitful. One might find oneself working alone in a position of responsibility in a non-Christian setting. Examples of teamwork would be, in the medical world, group practices or individual practices where one would have the appropriate assistants.

5. Manner of Life

(96) Members live in small groups in residences that are either rented or placed at their disposal. For a central house, see number 59. Wherever possible, an oratory should provide the opportunity for silent prayer and for the celebration of Vespers in common.

Living alone must be and must remain an exception. When it is absolutely necessary, the accommodation should not be too far from a group of the community, so that good contacts can be maintained.

(97) One member in each residence is its superior; her orders are to be followed.

(98) The general instructions concerning simplicity in accommodation, dress, and lifestyle must be made suitably specific in the women's branch (cf. no. 38).

(99) Each member must have a confessor, who, even if he is not a member of the community, is familiar with its spirit. Each member must give a regular account to the superior general of her spiritual life and all other important matters.

(100) The women's branch of the community must in a special way take seriously and try to put into action what was said above (no. 50) about forming a "contemplative core".

6. Leadership

(101) The whole branch is led by a superior general, who in turn is in contact with the clerical moderator of the Community of St. John.

(102) The superior has beside her a council of at least three members. This council must be consulted in all important decisions affecting the community or individual members. It can be expanded to include the superiors of the various residential communities. These report regularly on their particular area.

(103) Normally, the superiors of residential communities will change frequently. The superior general remains in office for a longer period.

(104) The leadership of the community does not include the advisers for certain of the professions. (These are women of extensive experience who advise others working in the same field when there are difficult cases concerning their profession and responsibilities.) However, as provided for in number 87, they can be referred to for advice in certain cases.

7. The Circle of Associates

(105) A wider circle of women, including married women, who feel attracted to the spirit of the community, can be regarded as belonging to it spiritually without actual membership. This circle can be invited to some of the events organized by the community. Some of the community's members will keep in contact with these interested persons, inform them of suitable publications and events, and be available to them if they pay a visit.

8. Departure and Dismissal

(106) The rules governing a member's leaving of the community are to be found in the special directives. When someone leaves the community, she should do so in such a way that she retains a positive relationship with the community. She should be helped to find her way in her new life.

The dismissal of a member by the superior general of the branch must be done with the consent of her council and after consultation with the priest-superior of the whole institute. Dismissal is possible even after final promises when a member has become totally estranged from the spirit of the community or has caused grave scandal.

D. THE MEN'S BRANCH

1. Spirituality

(107) Men who undertake to live according to the evangelical counsels as laymen should not imagine that things are harder for them than for priests, monks, or members of active orders. They can also take heart from those men who, from purely worldly motives, choose to remain unmarried, for example, for the sake of research. Obedience is no less strict in many business firms, and in the military, poverty can be felt no less keenly during certain kinds of expeditions (not to speak of the world's countless refugees) than where the counsels of Christ are adhered to for the sake of his work.

Moreover, men who want to follow this path should bear in mind how important it is to extend the life of the counsels into the secular sphere. To realize this we have only to consider the fact that very many people, who in the past would have gone to the priest for advice and absolution, today sit in the waiting rooms of doctors and psychiatrists. Teachers of secular subjects, to the best of their ability, may well be offering a substitute for the lack of, or for deficiencies in, religious instruction. Other professional people, too, such as lawyers, journalists, writers, publishers, and so on, these days more than in the past, need a power supply from the innermost resources of the Church.

(108) The case of the doctor, especially the psychotherapist, requires special consideration, because nowadays he

has to take the place of the priest in a far-reaching way. He ought to blend smoothly the natural knowledge and ethos of his profession with his Christian attitude to life and understanding of man. One should not exclude the possibility of a mental health specialist not merely collaborating with a priest but actually receiving priestly ordination, so that he can absolve his patient at the end of a course of treatment that has been conducted in a Christian manner. This would not necessarily involve the person in question having to move over to the priestly branch of the community. Our foundress did not think it would be out of the question for a male member to become a gynecologist. In her diaries she gave relevant instructions on this for medical students.

(109) Given what was said above about the relationship between the gospel and power, members should seek to hold positions from which they can exercise an effective apostolate for the sake of the Kingdom of God. However, at the same time, they should beware of chasing after jobs that are influential in worldly terms. When there is unavoidable conflict between worldly influence and Christian littleness, a look at the gospel will always decide the issue.

2. Admission

(110) For admission, the conditions laid down in numbers 20–27, 84, and 85 apply. The age limit, by contrast with that of women, can be raised somewhat, but only if there is still sufficient time for the practice of a profes-

sion. On entry, an opening up of conscience, covering the whole of one's previous life, is to be made before the superior of the men's branch. If the decision about the candidate's suitability is difficult, longer exercises (up to thirty days) should precede the decision.

3. Formation

(111) As in the women's branch, the choice of a profession should not be made independently of obedience within the community, so that the whole of one's work in the world may be protected and blessed by this obedience.

As in the other two branches, spiritual and theological formation should take place before professional training, assuming that the educational background of the person concerned, his understanding of the community ideal, and the need for testing his secular and spiritual aptitudes demand it. If professional work has already begun and, for cogent reasons, cannot be interrupted for a longer period of time, the introduction should take place alongside it. When this occurs, however, vacations and times of leave can be used for further formation in the spirit of community (but without damaging health).

Vigilance should be exercised to ensure that the spiritual foundations of the community, as explained in the directives, are correctly understood and assimilated and also that the theological formation is as thorough as possible. Subjects relevant only to priests will be omitted, but there must be mastery of everything necessary for theological conversations and discussions—including opinions that are found in the Church but are theologically inadequate —so that there is no danger of lapsing into a naïve fundamentalism.

This formation is to be carried out under the supervision of a sound theologian, wherever possible a member of the community, even if the person studying has to work for long periods on his own.

4. Promises

(112) First, temporary promises are made at the end of two years of formation and after a few days of retreat. They are repeated annually. Final promises are made only after a sufficient number of years of probation in the person's particular profession ("not less than five years", CIC 723, 2). A retreat of suitable duration and a general confession should precede these final promises.

5. Manner of Life

(113) Professions can be practiced on one's own or in a team. In the case of the latter, it is not necessary, though it is desirable, for the other people in the team to be members of the community. Likewise, members may live on their own or in small groups, but in any case they should meet together frequently for common prayer and for spiritual and social exchange.

6. Following the Counsels in Professional Life

(114) Evangelical poverty, which "all must love as a mother", will in many cases form the best criterion by which a male member can check that his conduct is in keeping with the counsels. In secular institutes, where the members normally earn money, the danger is even greater than in the monastic and other religious orders that the original spirit may be lost through the disregard of poverty, even when the prohibition of the hoarding of goods, as laid down in the directives, is correctly observed by the community's leadership. The individual must constantly ask himself how far, even taking into account the standard of living appropriate to his profession, he practices his profession purely for the love of God and neighbor. He must ask himself whether he regards his income as belonging not to himself but to the community, whether, in the general conduct of his life, he strives after unselfishness and moderation and does not shy away from experiencing, from time to time, the sharply felt effects of his promise of poverty.

(115) Each member will constantly examine himself to make sure that he is not treating his professional work as a self-contained world quite separate from obedience in the community and that he is absolutely ready to accept the admonition and, if necessary, the censure of his superiors and the comments of his brethren, especially about his personal conduct. Indeed, he must ask himself whether, in an extreme situation, he is ready to comply with the orders of the branch superior or of the moderator of the whole community (who will have come to an agreement

with their council about the matter) to move from his place of work or even to change his profession itself.

(116) As for celibacy, he will ask himself whether he has preserved the integrity of his original decision and attitude in the face of the different views held by his colleagues and many of his patients and clients. At the same time, of course, he will be sensitive to what other people regard as an obligation for them and not indiscreetly force his own views on them, especially in things which apply to him as a man dedicated in body and soul to God.

(117) If he is honest with himself in his daily examination of conscience, he will not find it hard to be honest in the account that he gives of his conscience to his superiors.

7. Leadership

(118) The leadership of the men's branch is in the hands of one superior. When the community expands more internationally, he can appoint subordinate directors for the individual regions and countries after he has discussed it with the outgoing superior, who will know the circumstances and recommendations of the regional members. As in the women's branch, he has a council beside him, which helps him with important decisions. If subordinate directors are appointed, the council will consist of them, of the administrators of important works (cf. no. 59), and a representative of the priests' branch. He, for his part, is one of the advisers of the priest who has the task of leading the whole community.

In line with what was said in number 32, it may be desirable for individual members to be appointed as special advisers for the individual professional branches.

8. Leaving the Community

(119) The same rules apply as above (no. 106).

III

APPENDIX:
THE EXERCISES AS
SEEN FROM HEAVEN

(Kerns, August 1950)

FOREWORD

The text added here as an appendix offers a further, very clear example of the "collaboration" between Adrienne and me. The modest task fell to me of giving the Exercises to our women's community, while Adrienne, at the wish of St. Ignatius and through my instrumentality as priest and spiritual director, for those few days received the extraordinary charism of listening to my conferences from the perspective of heaven and describing her impressions after each conference. One day in 1942, on her way back from the office, she saw a bright light shining in front of her car. (A man called out from the street: "Is something burning in that car?") At the same time she heard a voice: "*Tu vivras au ciel et sur la terre*" [You will live in heaven and on earth]. The truth of these words was subsequently confirmed on countless occasions. She was transferred to heaven, as a kind of guest, among all the angels and the blessed. She encountered them—this is typical of Adrienne—without shyness and in a spirit of friendship and then returned to her earthly affairs in an equally objective and realistic manner. At the same time, when her task required it, she recognized that she had a mediating position between heaven and earth. Thus, as far as Adrienne was concerned, there was nothing really extraordinary about the job she was given to do during these days nor about the introductory instructions from St. Ignatius about what exactly I had to do.

Finally, it should be noted that this extraordinary charism was without doubt bestowed with the future community in mind. The community will have to concern itself not merely with the practice and intimate knowledge of St. Ignatius' *Spiritual Exercises* but also with this "heavenly dimension", which shows everything—from the detachment of the "Principle and Foundation" to the concluding "*Suscipe*"—to be the definitive Christian attitude and thus the goal for which we strive. (Something of St. John is present embryonically in the *Exercises*—as Christology, but also as the life of the Church placed between Mary and Peter, "Christ's true Bride, our holy Mother, the hierarchical Church".)

TEXT

Instruction: "Father [St. Ignatius] would like to say a few things that are only indirectly concerned with the Exercises, but will have a significance for later introductions and exercises. He would like Adrienne to be sent to heaven for the next few days. H. U. must do this and let Adrienne share the Exercises with him from heaven. After each conference, she must give a short commentary on how things look from there, in the light of the Trinity. With this in mind, on each occasion, H. U. should take her out of heaven for, say, a quarter of an hour and ask her questions. He can think up all kinds of questions; from time to time, he can also ask her what she would like to speak about. Once in a while she will speak spontaneously. In her superabundant visions much will emerge that is useful for both of them, as well as for later Exercises and for general practical and theoretical consideration.

"Let her make her confession twice. The first time invite her to go to confession before she thinks of it. Do a kind of mirror confession: pose problems and see how she sees herself in them. The second time let her confess spontaneously. Take careful note of these confessions. (Possibly make notes.) If he wants to, H. U. can call upon SP [*Sanctus Pater* = St. Ignatius] if there is something he does not understand or wants to know.

"In the vision of heaven, pay special attention to how the things of this world, the children of this world, look to Adrienne. She will also share in a large part of the confessions of other people. From where she is, she can go almost anywhere she thinks necessary, or where H. U. thinks she should go. H. U. has therefore a certain power over heaven, which later, when A. no longer returns, will be important for him.

"Father blesses both of them. He is, of course, at their side and takes part in everything that concerns them. They are in total union with him, and he watches over their foundations. Anything negative, anything that does not come off, must always be seen as a learning experience, never as an estrangement from Father. Father is glad to be allowed to help his children."

The Introductory Mass

Usually, when I meet saints in heaven, each one is by himself; only rarely are there groupings and processions and such like. But during Holy Mass they all come together to form a kind of sphere, and each saint is inclined toward Mass on earth, as if heaven were joining together around the Mass . . . in the direction of God. All the citizens of heaven turn their hearts toward the Event from which they receive joy and delight—the heart is the seat of delight—but of course this takes place in the self-giving Lord, in union with him. For example, at the Offertory they all unite themselves with him who offers and is offered. Each is in his proper place, but all are arranged in orderly fashion in the light of the Trinity, the very cause of the arrangement. When you're trying to take a group photograph, one that will be clearly just that, the photograph of a group, you don't want everybody picking his own place; no, you want everyone to be willing to fit in with the plan you have made. In the same way, the triune God keeps heaven compactly together during Mass. At other times I have seen an individual saint in his relationship with the Mass. Now, though, it is different. All of the saints form together a sort of atmosphere, a coloration, a perfume, directed toward what is happening in the Mass. The Mother of God is also at the center of all this.

Man is Created for God, to Praise Him, Reverence Him, and Serve Him

I have forgotten what kind of human being I am. I am with you as you speak of man and say that man has been created "for" something, but at the same time I am up above, looking down on earth and earthly striving. I notice something: to understand this fundamental principle, the unity of heaven cannot remain closed; it has to open itself up, because man is on his way toward it. Sin interferes with the direct course of man's striving, and so it is hard to imagine the unity. Where shall we begin?

The best way is to start with the Trinity. When I see the unity of heaven in the light of the Trinity, I can understand it. Seen from below, because of sin, the unity is incomprehensible; I can only try and piece together the individual fragments. But I can have the consolation of knowing that, despite everything, the unity does exist. And all at once I realize why there are apparitions coming out of heaven, and why St. Thérèse of Lisieux makes her roses rain upon earth. All this comes from the unity

of heaven, to strengthen man on earth in his belief that
there really is this unity.

Man is created for the praise, reverence, and service
of God. In heaven these three things are completely intertwined. God saw that the world he had created in all
its multiplicity was good, but he himself is everything
together, perfect unity. And we only feel the multiplicity
because sin has estranged us from the unity. In heaven
there is no need for a distinction between praise, reverence, and service. The Gifts of the Holy Spirit are also basically just *one* gift. The praise of God lies already within
the goodness of creaturely becoming and being, and reverence and service are contained there too.

When one human being really loves another, his own
faults seem to him like stains on that love; they detract
from the unity of love in and with the Beloved. The
Beloved also recognizes the faults of the other, because
they are opposed to their common love. When there is
genuine love, the Lover starts with a statement of praise
about the Beloved: "You are wonderful." For the time
being, those words contain everything; the specific reasons for the statement come later. When the Lover speaks
about the Beloved with someone who does not know her,
needless to say he has to begin with all the specifics, until gradually a unified picture emerges. Every statement
we make, whether it refers to a human being we love or
to God, means more than what lies directly within it. It
points in a certain direction, but it cannot show the end
of the road: that is reverence. God is greater than all we
can attribute to him by way of praise. But love does not
stop at praise. It wants to serve the Beloved with all its

powers, to show him what befits him on account of his glory.

Man and Other Things on Earth

Man's task on earth is not himself alone nor God alone, but the building of a bridge between man and God, and the building bricks are the things of this world. When a man really lives out the task he has received from God, he constructs something holy out of the world, like a church or cathedral. A real cathedral, in all its finished beauty, is an image of heaven and the order of heaven. It is a concrete example of what the "Principle and Foundation" [in the Exercises] mean. It makes clear what praise, reverence, and service are: man's response to being created by God. As an image of heaven, the cathedral exists to take men into itself for the praise of God. It is a symbol of the Church founded by our Lord, which is in turn an image of the order of heaven. It is within that order that the saints and the office of priesthood can be understood more clearly. Man, created good by God, can use the good creation to make an instrument that will amplify his voice and enable him to give God an answer in full. If he really follows the instructions he has been given, the structures he confers on the world correspond to what heaven expects from him.

In the temporal course of history, the work of completing the cathedral goes on—beginning with the Fathers, continuing with St. Augustine, St. Thomas, and countless others: each one takes up from where the others have left off. When sin intervenes, there can be contradictions: one man contradicts what his predecessor said. But new truth can emerge even from contradiction, when the work of construction is done, not in self-will, but in love of the truth. Of course, were we not sinners, our theological reflections would be briefer, more concentrated, more unified, and would lead more swiftly to their goal.

Heaven looks upon the growing response of the world, at the "merit" of struggling mankind. We must both use the things of this world and leave them alone, take them up but also give them up, eat and fast. Anyone pursuing a goal has to renounce everything else for the sake of that goal. And there are many things that we have to leave where they are, so that others can pick them up.

The world's response to God emerges, like a cathedral, as a complete whole. It has tiny spires and oriels, which are hardly noticeable and yet an essential part of the whole. So it is with the small renunciations that we make.

The Time of the Exercises

There is a constant encounter between the precise sentence you are speaking, or whatever else is happening in this world, and its counterpart in heaven. The "Now" does not lose its value in the Eternal, even though there, in temporal terms, it is an "Ever Now". A Christian idea is uttered in time and is incorporated into the truth of the Trinity. That truth subsisted unchanged beforehand and will subsist unchanged afterward, and yet it is open and receptive to what you are saying right now. God wants his trinitarian light to be given a special prominence in this very statement. When the statement is made, its meaning is revealed in heaven. We can compare it to a light coming on in a large ticket office when someone presses a certain button. This lighting up is proof of the correctness of the statement, the truth of which was already validated in heaven. But for the earthly mission to be fulfilled, the statement must be made in the way that corresponds to the light of the Trinity. There is an element of prayer in this correspondence, a security that comes from being guided, a confirmation that we are on the right track.

Detachment

In the eyes of heaven, detachment is the eradication of what God does not want. In the exchanges of the three Divine Persons, in the interchange of the saints in heaven, each person is open to the other in such a way that it is always only God's complete will that is done. If Mary is so full of graciousness, if she moves with such incomparable beauty, it is clear that, in so doing, she corresponds totally with God's will. (Someone might dance for God; a beautiful dancer could express God.) Mary's graciousness and her wonderful movements are a praising of God and an exact response to the task with which God has entrusted.

If everyone on earth were detached, it would be just like that. But people who are really detached on earth form only small islands. These need to be enlarged. Of course, there is resistance from the world, which wants to do its own will. The actions of people who are detached are taken up into heavenly truth but not into the sphere of those who do not want to do the will of God.

Adrienne Briefly Brought Back from Heaven

Being in heaven is not like a dream, because dreams do not have so much reality. The obedience that put me there can do anything. The going up and down is symptomatic. Obedience always intensifies human possibilities in a very vigorous way, taking them into the supernatural. It is as if an apartment, a place for making music, were being enlarged. Obedience is like a stimulant for the soul. It moves a person to places which the disobedient does not even know exists. If someone says to me, "Have a go at this or that", I may say, "I can't." But if it is imposed on me in obedience, my capacity for achievement increases enormously. The possibility of my bringing it off is very different from my own estimate of my powers. The source of weakness to be found in my doubts and refusals is extinguished. Achieving something in obedience has nothing to do with latent powers (Coué). We are admitted to a world that otherwise, without obedience, would remain closed. I do not awaken a latent power within me because I want to obey. No, obedience brings it to me. It is *un apport de l'obéissance* [the contribution of obedience]. And it does not bring it to me personally. It is part of the obedience which the Son gave the Father. It is also somehow a proof of the truth of God that the Son, who brought this power into the world, should have made it accessible to the world, so much so, in fact, that we can avail ourselves of it today.

Seen from heaven, human beings look like numbers: they are open to the eyes of all. You can see the connections between the things they say: true and false, lies, and so forth. At the same time their wretchedness is apparent, because you can see how much God's grace does in them, and also because they grope their way through the world like blind men. Then there is the distance between heaven and earth. You cannot simply break off and intervene. You might want to spend your heaven appearing on earth. But if you're going to appear, on the other side there has to be the capacity to see. You can't say that God should have created more seers. There is a mystery here that is impenetrable, even in heaven. I once heard a saint calling out to a man: "Hey, hey, hey!" The man made a movement, as if he were trying to swat a fly, and then went on his way.

It cannot be said that heaven is sad because men do so much that is wrong. It is, so to speak, gripped by the greater meaning that lies hidden in God. Lovers are not angry with each other because one does something the other does not understand. The annoyance of not understanding immediately dissolves into love: "I'm sure you know why you're doing that." And God knows why he permits something, and the citizens of heaven are made privy to this permission, so that no sadness arises, even though there may be grounds for sadness. They see sin and do not praise it, but they also see the greatness of God's plan, which is worthy of praise.

Can we say that they are impeded in their beatitude? I don't want to say that it's a matter of indifference to them. They understand evil, but they refrain from evaluating it, because God's love is predominant. It is a form of obedience. The ultimate mystery of sin lies hidden in God. He created a world in which there is temptation.

On Prayer

In heaven, silence and speech are so intertwined that they can hardly be distinguished. The Son is silent in order to speak with the Father, and yet he also finds words for this conversation. It is like the rests in a piece of music. The rests are the dying away of what has been said and the introducing of what is going to be said. In fact, were there no silence, the words could not be understood. Whether the Son speaks or is silent, it is to the greater glory of the Father. We see immediately that both things are equally true.

We pray best when we are taken into the speaking silence and the silent speaking of heaven, of God himself. We should not make too sharp a distinction but just look to God. Prayer is like a kiss, like the lingering of the kiss already given and the anticipatory joy of the kiss to come. It is all the same in prayer, just as it is all the same in love.

Vocal prayer has its rest in the form of contemplative prayer, and vice versa. The whole of prayer is a being and a becoming. It is always word and answering word. It happens and lets things happen. This is where the unceasingness of prayer comes from. It is like the Father eternally begetting the Son, and so on. It is impossible to say whether in love the question or the answer is more important. When God asks and man answers, the answer is already included within the question.

Meditation on Sin (1)

The triune God in the dialogue of love: Everything is fulfilled. But there are some influences close to us that are constantly interrupting. They cannot be ignored. What is said is incomprehensible, but it is stubborn and presumptuous and cannot be dismissed. They speak against us: that is their theme. Against our love, against what we do in love, and with such persistence that you would think they were paid to disturb our love and our dialogue.

It is unanswered. God knows that God loves and that his love is stronger than all hate and all meddling. And yet he is disturbed. Although from the outset he has conquered it, this hate disturbs him. Not in the way it would disturb men in their love, because men are always individuals, separate, whereas for God men are components of his divine love, despite their hate. Components insofar as they *are*, not insofar as they hate. God created them for the Son, and the Son has rescued them for the Father. They are not something alien, something tertiary, but the creatures of divine love.

The Mother of God and the saints are the ones who could do it. For the triune God, they are a "super-consolation" for the "disconsolation" that defective love gives him. They are always invited to participate in the dialogue within God, but also in the dialogue with men, because they are proofs and mediators of the love of God, and God tells them what they have to say to men. Of course, every man has direct access to God, but we should pay attention to this mediation which God has established. What the mediator communicates to God is a consolation to him. The loving mediators, so to speak, direct God's attention, disturbed by sinners, toward his good work. If you give me a novel to read, you won't like it if I put it aside and perhaps after twenty years deign to read it. The same is true of every gift. That is why God likes his mediators to function, because they praise his good work and experience in their own lives the overcoming of sin.

What became apparent was the way in which heaven took defensive measures against sin. Not the reactions of individual saints, but the defensive measures in their totality.

The troubadour fights during the day for his lady, but then in the evening he is at her side and sings her his poems. It is part of the tenderness of her love that he should be strong and combative. She shudders when she thinks of the dangers to which he exposes himself for her sake, but her love can contain the shuddering. This is an analogy for understanding how the dialogue of love between Father, Son, and Spirit is carried on, even though it is constantly concerned with sinners. None of the offenses we commit against God can interrupt his dialogue of love. No human comparison from the world of human love can do justice to the tenderness and the toughness of this relationship.

Meditation on Sin (2)

This part is one of the specialties of St. Ignatius: opening ourselves to God through our consciousness of sin. It is strange how, now he is in heaven, he turns, so to speak, away from God toward sinners, whenever good retreats are taking place. So actively engaged is he, so much is he in his element, that the retreatant's sin becomes an occasion for turning to God.

In this meditation the whole of heaven is turned toward the retreatants, but in a different way from yesterday at Mass. Here there is a phase of what one might call "rigidification", of total incomprehension of sin. It appears first of all as something heaven cannot cope with. It is the opposite of our invocation and veneration of the saints. Often we invoke them and receive no reply. But likewise the saints and angels call to us, and from us sinners they receive no reply. Then follows a kind of takeover of the two parties by the triune God. Everything vanishes into the mystery of his invisibility. One would like to think that the Son is inspired by this to create the treasury of the Church's prayer. It is a result of the *communio sanctorum*, of the common imploring of God to overcome sin.

There is such a thing as personal sin, and it has an effect on other people. Let us suppose that the Exercises have been given falsely. The retreat master speaks for himself, not for God. If this were the case, he would be committing a personal sin and would be guilty of the fact that the retreatants were persisting in their sins. Something like this can happen between a pastor and his parish, or between a public official and the people who live in his district. Say someone wanted to rouse himself from his half-heartedness, but his confessor told him: "Everything is in order. Don't exaggerate!" Again, in this case he would be sinning personally and would be guilty of the common sin, in which every sinful and half-hearted person shares.

In heaven this "organization" of sin has its opposite: personal sanctity and common sanctity. On All Saints' Day or in the Litany of the Saints, we venerate this common sanctity or invoke the individual saints in their commonness. After the Litany we do not ask ourselves whether we invoked one saint more than another. Thus in heaven, alongside the personal qualities of the saints, there is a certain self-effacement, the very opposite of the collectivity and "impersonality" of sin that is dominant on earth. Like is repaid with like.

Whenever there is talk of sin, the Son can be seen standing before the Father. I can't really say that I don't see the Father, because I don't notice that I am not seeing him. The Son, whom I do see and with whom I speak, he sees the Father.

Adrienne's Confession in Heaven

When you confess in heaven, you can't do it as this individual person. I have to confess not just as one woman on her own, but as a human being: as a human being who bears much responsibility for the whole world; as someone who at the moment does not see her faults and failings with sufficient plasticity, even though she tries to recognize them, because they have gone so far into the plasticity of other people's that what is mine or yours or his points to something that is "ours" in a very broad sense. I should like to use this fact to excuse or extricate myself, but I can't find myself, and I think I am not supposed to look for myself. I, the human being, have committed every sin against God. But I, Adrienne, and I, the woman living the consecrated life, must confess for the world, for myself, for religious (not women), because in heaven I have a special responsibility for religious, or rather a special connection, *connexité*. But in this confession time is done away with. I do not confess what I did in some form or other twenty or a hundred years ago, but what I am doing at present, I the human being and I the woman living the consecrated life, and I Adrienne. I confess right now from earth, which is immersed in eternity and in which it is necessary to take account of the world of today. Today in the world, but not just today in the calendrical sense, but a broader today embracing perhaps many years.

Confession: I have committed every half-hearted prayer, every prayer forgotten to be said, all lack of love for God, even willed paganism. . . . And I confess—but as a kind of delegate—the sins we committed together and the sins that perhaps other people do not see and do not want to confess. This is something much more serious than if, in a regular confession, I were to include other people's sins, which were not committed by me just now. I confess not only infidelity to the gospel, to Christian doctrine, but also the way it has not been observed as a rule. And rule here can mean each of the rules of the various religious orders. The Holy Spirit of God is offended by this bad performance.

I must also confess the distance. Being so much in heaven, I see how we constantly increase the distance. I the human being, I the Catholic, I the believer, I the religious. When I think of God, I situate him far too deep. I assign him a position that reduces my distance from him, and, in so doing, I increase that distance immeasurably.

I confess all lack of love for neighbor. This lack has very precise forms. It goes from complete contempt to (from heaven's point of view we cannot talk like this) the slightest neglect. But this is a human concept, which, seen from heaven, appears, as through a magnifying glass, enlarged, ramified, willed.

Repentance . . . O yes, I repent . . . and I see repentance quite differently from usual. I repent as human being, as religious, as mediator. However, because I have been invited to be in heaven, I am somehow enveloped in a coating that robs me of my control of my feelings if they were of a personal nature. Repentance is transplanted into the Cross. It is now, not something going from me to the Cross, but something given from the Cross to me, not something of my own, but something belonging to the Lord. It is more a doing away with sin in the Lord than what the word "repentance" usually denotes.

Intention. It is large and comprehensive. One is vigorously taken up into the Father. The intention has the quality of reality, feasibility, the capacity to be translated into life: it *will* be carried out. Usually, when I resolve to improve myself, I know in advance that I shall do it and not do it. When I look into my heart and inmost being, I have to admit I do not believe it. Now, though, I do believe. Because I see the intention in others, in the saints, in the heavenly. As a power that is intrinsic to the truth of confession. I see that the saints are all resolved to help sinners to carry out the intention made in their confession. Vianney is of paramount importance here. Because even

on earth he achieved such resolution and commitment
and repentance. He personally repents, with bitter tears,
of the sins that this murderer, of whom he knew nothing five minutes ago, committed perhaps twenty years
ago when he killed a negro in the jungle, and at the moment of confession he becomes the penitent's brother,
for whom he bears responsibility. In heaven they really
do *bear* responsibility. But they bear it in the visibility of
grace.

Were I not now at the same time in heaven, I would
confess that I am responsible for every sin. I would repent
of every one of them and form the intention to commit
none of them ever again. In heaven are all those who help
with the bearing of responsibility and change the quality
of what the sinner recognizes as guilt. You know you're
responsible, and yet at the same time you're relieved of
a certain responsibility. Otherwise heaven would be unbearable. Without this relief, you would swear: "I must
go back to earth and take everyone with me." You would
say: "How much more effective I would be if I could set
myself up in the market place and start preaching instead
of living here in heaven!" This relief from responsibility
means appointment to a different kind of responsibility,
which is meant to become a reality in the humility of
divine worship. This humility is given in such a way that
a person completely abstains from making a judgment
about the efficacy of the new responsibility. It must be
enough to see that it leads to God, that he holds all the
threads in his hand.

Absolution? . . . I really should like to receive absolution. I realize that the value of the sacrament applies in

heaven as well. Seen in that light, prayer, too, is sacramental, with an effect in heaven, and from heaven it has an effect on earth. If you can absolve me, it will have an effect on earth. It will have an effect on me, when I return to the world, but also, by the mysterious law of the Church's treasury on earth, it will have an effect on other sinners. If you let me make my confession in heaven, I think you will want a greater confession and a stronger absolution.

Do the other saints confess with me? The Mother of God? The angels? Yes, they confess with me. If you invoke St. Ignatius, he comes without breaking his connection with the other saints.

(After absolution.) You have the ministerial power to absolve. It comes to you from heaven and leads into heaven. Looking from heaven, I see more clearly that there is basically very little that is personal about absolution. If you absolve someone who has committed murder, this absolution touches, to a very small degree, the person who has not confessed. You set something free for the forgiveness of the sin of someone who does not acknowledge his sin. That is what "absolving people into heaven" means. Heaven takes up the sacramental power and distributes it as it sees fit. It is no more mysterious than anything else that is authentic. Everything that is authentic comes from heaven and goes to heaven, and it is subject to a law that God alone knows.

The World and Concupiscence

Through concupiscence I seek what pleases me; what pleases God comes at best in second place. But God tries to convince us that we should first seek his joy and only in his find our own. God takes pleasure in the world. He wants to see in it the closeness of his Son.

From every man a thread leads to God. But men confuse all the threads, and so their relationship with God is disturbed. If someone wants to point his thread straight toward God, but other people confuse him, and he does not know the way to God, he has no chance of wriggling his way out. But if someone knows God and the way to God, he can disentangle himself, and then, as I said earlier, he has responsibility for others.

While God and his saints look upon this confusion, the rightness of the saints' relationship with God is revealed. They look at God and want to experience only what comes from God. During this meditation, the saints behave in a remarkable way. For the sake of the world, they totally disappear; they do not show their faults, their bad example. And yet they are also the first in line to comfort men who want to escape from their concupiscence. They step back, so that they do not encourage any sinner in his sin. And yet at the decisive moment they step forward to show him that conversion really is possible. (The reason for this is that concupiscence is so strong in man that he would like to find the sinner in the saint.)

All the threads come together in the center that is God. First in the Father, not in Christ. This gives you the feeling that you really are seeing God—even though you don't see the Father directly.

Adrienne's Confession between Heaven and Earth

(The other retreatants have just made their confession.) During the confessions of the others, I felt myself in conflict. I had to be there in the confessions, but at the same time I had to be with those who had meanwhile visited me. I heard a few words from the confessions, while I was talking with the visitors (the Prioress of Bethany). Where these words were concerned, I always had the feeling: "This is my word, too." The confessions I overheard were all honest, so each time I was, as it were, comforted. But in the comfort there was also discomfort. I felt uncomfortable with the fact that, even though I am a sinner, I was being allowed to be in heaven. These confessions made me feel like a sinner in heaven. I am in solidarity with earth without being in conflict with heaven. I was perhaps like someone, newly arrived in heaven, who as yet cannot take it in.

Now there is an involvement of the inhabitants of heaven in the confession of sins on earth which enables *me* to experience sin differently. My personal sin. Faced with the prodigality of God's love for me (and in heaven I can see this prodigality with particular clarity), I realize how little I do for him. In heaven I learn how much grace there is in my earthly life (the many apparitions, and so on). And from heaven I see that I do not match up enough, and I think, "If the children had a better mother, they would make better confessions." I see my lack of love, of prayer, of effectiveness. But I don't see this because I see *myself* from heaven but because I see *sin* from heaven. When I say in confession on earth that I do not love enough, I know something quite specific about myself. But when I say something from heaven, then I recognize it in its effect, because somehow my confession enters into the confession of my children; my lack of love shows itself in them. I am consoled (because I live in the mercy of God) and unconsoled (because I have never or only rarely seen so clearly how little I match up). This conflict comes, of course, from the fact that I am not yet in heaven in a definitive way. Once we are there definitively, we are absolved definitively.

Contemplation of the Call and Kingdom of Christ

In heaven you suddenly realize how everything fits together: the Lord calls us to follow him, so that we can enter with him into the glory of the Father. This entry into glory is always an experience shared with him. When you enter, you see where all the preceding stages were leading. Nothing is discarded. Everything has its place—in this entry into the Father's glory.

We are expected to be satisfied with the same food as the King, to share with him the same strains and night watches. And the whole of heaven shares, too. There is something very similar to the wrath of the Father: the Father's anxiety about the Son. The Father created the world in joy, in a kind of carefree way, like an artist who wants to produce a painting of the greatest beauty for his son. But the colors he works with are fading, and his son meanwhile has grown up and thinks the painting is so beautiful that he wants to become a painter, too, in order to emulate it, and so he takes up what remains of his father's colors. The father is worried: you should use more robust colors. . . . The son's intention moves him, and yet it frightens him that the son is so much in love with this of all pictures. . . . This analogy is weak, but it does point to something hidden in the heart of the Father. A human father may be anxious when he sees how his wife suffers in giving birth to their child and for a long time afterward is in poor health. Did he do something wrong? He is innocent, and yet somehow he feels guilty. . . . Again the analogy is weak. And yet who can imagine what goes on in the heart of God the Father while the Son is completing the work of redemption? The freedom he gave his creatures was the best thing he could have given them, but, after they have sinfully misused it, the question is unavoidable: Would it not have been better to withhold this freedom from them? And now the Son of God himself goes into the world and will get to feel the consequences of freedom's misuse: Should he have been allowed to go? The Father needs consolation, and the saints and angels, the whole of heaven, are a comfort to him: a visible result of a creation that despite everything is a success.

On the Incarnation

The perspective of heaven is reversed. Your eye does not travel from the widest and farthest, the edge of the globe, to the narrowest and nearest—to Mary and her overshadowing. No, the farthest thing is the overshadowing, then comes Mary, then the edge of the globe.

We say so lightly: God alone is the absolute, everything else is relative. But if the absolute God creates a world and a creature like man, then his action and its object also have an absolute character. Man is not a relative man, and God does not find his work to be relatively good. The world is limited, but that does not mean that it has no access to the divine and absolute, that it is cut off from it. It exists in conformity to God's will, and that conformity in its own way is perfect. It is only disturbed by sin. Only then does finitude escape from its relationship with God and lose its content and, like an emptied balloon, become a mere wrapping. From this moment on, the heavenly is the only absolute, and the contemplation, as St. Ignatius presents it, shows this: from the sphere where everything is harmonious you look on the world as on a realm of disharmony.

And then, at a precise point in time, the harmony is restored. The seed of God makes Mary fruitful, and from her the harmony spreads out through Galilee to the ends of the earth. In the overshadowing and only in the over- shadowing lie all the fullness and absoluteness of the heav- enly; there alone lies the standard by which the entire world is judged and measured. In the Incarnation the orig- inal harmony between God and the world is not only re- stored but enhanced, because God puts his very own seed into the womb of a human being through the Holy Spirit. At the overshadowing the whole triune God bows low over the Mother. The Son is not released by God into the world. The whole Godhead accompanies him and thus establishes the most intimate connection between God and world, heaven and earth. The world more than ever participates in the absoluteness of God.

The Mysteries of Christ's Childhood and Youth

In heaven, Mary—as the Mother of the Son, the Virgin, the human being in whom God and world meet—is always to the fore when God carries out his plans in the world. She is to the fore in two ways: passively, as an example showing how God typically acts, but also actively, because she, who on earth was contemplative, in heaven unfolds her activity. In heaven most of the saints have primarily a contemplative attitude, and when actions are demanded of them—for example, when St. Anthony was called—their contemplation feeds their actions, the actions fall back on the prayer, on their vision of God, their contemplative act. But Mary on earth was the perfect contemplative, and she becomes active only to make visible her contemplation. When she speaks or prays the Magnificat, she reveals only her interior contemplative attitude. In heaven her earthly contemplation is so deeply inserted into the activity of God that she becomes a "co-agent" with God, and she does so in the very spirit of her earthly contemplation. Through the earthly contemplation she became capable of this heavenly action. The other saints live in a tranquility, almost a poverty of movement. They simply undergird and underline what the Blessed Mother does. Indeed, in a certain way, the Son himself seems to renounce the continuation of his

earthly action, so that the perpetually active being of his
Mother should become more prominent.

Here the Spirit appears in a new light. He blows where
he wills. But he commits himself wherever someone with
real faith and humility is ready for him. Of course, he
commits himself above all to the Blessed Mother, because this is part of his original mission, and she who
is most humble is also the most ready for him. As "pre-
redeemed", she always welcomes him spiritually and is
thereby empowered to receive him bodily. Thus the Holy
Spirit meets himself in her. The Spirit who took charge
of her spirit receives from that spirit of hers the permission to take charge of her body, so that his most extreme
capacities meet in her. (Here is a human analogy: the love
between a man and a woman can be so total in spirit that
when the man desires bodily union, the woman grants
it.) Thus Mary is in plenitude the *Sponsa Christi* and can
be imitated as such by the religious sister. A religious vocation is a following of the body with respect to the spirit,
in a contemplative or active life. The person who follows
Christ is so moved in spirit that he allows his body to
give its response to the call. His Yes is his action. He
sends his body into Carmel. Mary consigned her body to
the service of Christ and remained contemplative (that is
how her contemplation became visible), and so in heaven
she takes hold of the action that results from this contemplation and becomes the source of the greatest activity in
the Church. In her the Church responds to her Lord truly
as Bride.

When this happens, the prerogative of the Spirit clearly
emerges. He was the first person to take the Mother by

the hand at the Incarnation, to guide her earthly contemplation and now her heavenly action. She stands between the Father and the Son through him, through him as the Spirit of Love. Thus the prerogative of the Spirit becomes a prerogative of the Mother, in the sense that one can now discern in her the way in which the relationships between the Divine Persons take place. The perpetual actuality of the Incarnation can only be represented as a perpetual becoming man in the Mother. And the Spirit's hovering over the face of the waters at the beginning becomes concretely visible when he overshadows the Mother. When he takes the Mother as his partner, his spiritual nature is demonstrated to the whole of heaven. And this is how it must be shown and explained to those earthlings who, as I am now, have been sent into heaven. It is a very precise instruction in the form of a vision. Whoever sees it is sent back to earth with clear concepts. By way of example, it is demonstrated in the person of the Mother, who begins with contemplation and is now active in heaven.

There is a *spiritualité céleste*, a heavenly attitude on the part of the Spirit. The Spirit governs according to his nature and directs all things toward the Father, and he does so in a moved and mobile way. One of the strangest things about being in heaven is that, when we look at the spirituality of an individual saint on earth, we see in him a particular doctrine: certain things he approves, others he rejects. he has his preferences, his temperament, his struggles with his environment. Even though he has the wish to be open to God and to let the holy Spirit blow where he wills, there is a narrowing of the range of his spirituality: somehow he ties himself down. In heaven, however, the incorporation of everything into one's own spirituality is not limiting. The openness of heaven is so vast that in no way can it be narrowed. All that seems to be fixed—for example, looking at the Father, turning toward God through the Spirit—takes place within a movement, a blowing of the Spirit. In heaven, if for a moment you turn your eyes toward something, so that you can concentrate on it, you notice that the fixing only happens for the sake of an opening. Within the divine vitality all things are correspondingly mobile. If you look at a saint in heaven who is contemplating the Father or showing something that we recognize, you realize that he is under the influence of the divine life, of the Spirit, of the eternity of heaven. It is not really he himself who is showing and reflecting the thing, but rather God is doing the showing in him. He has become a representation of God. You see this representation when you look at him, and so he fulfills his task of being God's image, his likeness in the eternal blowing of the Spirit.

When we enjoy the evening twilight, we notice that it is essentially on the move. The situation of five minutes ago and the situation in five minutes' time are part of what is going on now. Movement gives relief. Something lights up which just a little while ago was not shining. If the scene were static, it would soon weary us. Heaven is essentially movement. Movement only becomes rigid for sinners on earth. It no longer annoys us. We have got used to it. When God the Father was walking in Paradise, he produced a breeze. He walked in the blowing wind.

The Narrative of the Temptations

At the time of Eve's temptation, there was such harmony between her and God—after all, the first human beings had only just come forth from the creative hands of God —that in a certain sense God entered into temptation with Eve. God knows what temptation means. He could enter the state of being tempted, share the experience of listening to the insinuating serpent, of questioning the prohibition, of imagining biting into the apple. He could go so far with them that the serpent's arguments would be granted a certain plausibility, though, in the light of authentic truth, that plausibility would be seen as false and mendacious.

The counterpart of this is the Lord's being guided into temptation by the devil. The Lord lets himself be tempted by the devil as long as God was able to accompany Eve into temptation. But in Paradise the distancing of man from God began when man let himself be led by the serpent on *his* way. Now the Lord goes this way in the company of the devil to show Adam where he should have turned back, the point at which the distancing began. In a sense, letting himself be accompanied by the devil is already distancing. God's answer will be the abandonment of the Son on the Cross: the distancing of the Father from the Son. In the life of our Lord there is a correspondence between everything: in this case, between the temptations and the Cross. And just as the Father trembles during the Son's temptations, so the Son trembles on the Cross when he is forsaken by the Father.

During the temptations the Son shows the Father once

more that his creation is good, and that man is good. It is an abstraction to say that the Son could not have sinned. True, the danger that makes the Father tremble is not in the Son but in the devil, who is anything but harmless. To meet him, to converse with him, is dangerous for any human being. And when the Son stops the devil, he is in the middle of real danger, a genuine struggle.

In heaven this can be seen best in the relationship of God and the saints. Any of the saints could have fallen, and some of them did. And God trembled for them, as he did for Adam and for the Son. But the saints did not really perceive this trembling, even when they did not fall. Perhaps they thought more of the wrath of God than of the trembling of God. Or they refrained from sin, because they thought of God or of his law, his providence; they were devoted to something else.

It is also in this way that the Son's bearing of temptation resembles his bearing of sin. On the Cross he will get to know the burden of sin; now he gets to know the devil's power of attraction. He *wants* to let himself be attracted by the devil's arguments, to be accompanied by the devil, in order to get to know the situation of man. The devil who tempts him is the same one who tempts man. Experiencing this situation is part of the Son's experience of the world. When he heals the woman with a flow of blood, in the miracle he gets to know the burden of sickness for the woman. He does not work his miracles from outside the human situation. It is not as if he first considers the gravity of the woman's sickness and then comes to the conclusion that he ought to set her free from this burden. No, he feels that God wants the miracle that is to take place to be accomplished and that the power that goes forth from him is the price that has to be paid: from this price he estimates the weight carried by the woman. When he fasts in the wilderness for forty days, in order to have the experience of temptation, he, so to speak, wipes the slate clean. He makes himself empty in order to experience the devil in the pure presence of God. He thereby opens up for us the way to making our life's decision, our choice of a state of life: the decision must be made in solitude, in voluntary separation from all other things, in prayer, but also in a new encounter with temptation. The devil who does the tempting before the choice of a state of life in the Exercises is the kind who adorns himself in the glamour of the world. The manifold experiences of our previous life do not daunt him. We are talking here of a radical Yes or No. All the small decisions made up to this point, during the thirty years of our Lord's life, are eliminated.

Three Modes of Humility, Two Standards

The third mode of humility is accomplished by our Lord when he bears the shame of the Cross. Through the third, the first and second modes become possible for men. When he became man, the Son had in mind the third level with respect to the Father, for only through the Cross does it become possible for man to attain any level of humility.

But the sentiments of the Son in the Incarnation reveal not only his own attitude but also that of the whole triune God. This becomes humanly clear through the Incarnation. The Son reveals himself, but he does so in order to glorify the Father and to manifest the Spirit. He reveals the Father and the Spirit before he reveals himself. And when he reveals himself, he does so in his openness to the Father in the Spirit, in his love for him. And in the Son's love for man appears the Father's love for his world, a love so great that it tolerates even the humiliation of the Son on the Cross, his bearing of all the transgressions of men.

Humiliation and confession belong together. On the Cross the Son lets himself be humiliated in order to confess everything that can and must be confessed. And he does this in a public confession, which manifests to us on the Cross every sin. Then he dies, and that death is a revelation of new life, which is given in a new way to us, who are created by God's life and redeemed by his Son's death. He dies and in so doing reveals our misused life, but at the same time he makes it free for regeneration, for a stunning new vitality.

(Seen from heaven, all earthly life seems different. Eternal life is not only its goal, to be attained somehow through death, but also the source from which it unceasingly draws. Earthly life is lived from within, in the midst of, eternal life. In heaven I am a guest, a guest who must not be afraid of being thrown out, a guest who does not understand the customs of the host. I am at home, and so I must not separate heavenly from everyday life. There is interaction between the two. Here below we are privileged to feed on the strength of heaven, but heaven also expects us to give it our own vitality and strength.)

Meditation on Scripture in Heaven

Heaven is always the eternal life between the Persons of the Trinity. Then comes the world and the disappointment of sin, and then the life and sacrifice of the Son. The whole of heaven *pays homage* in the Holy Spirit to this life and sacrifice. This homage of heaven is communicated to the world, because the Holy Spirit tells the apostles and the evangelists of the events in a way that they could never have formulated themselves. For a moment, the vividness of the Son's self-portrayal withdraws, so to speak, to make room for the vividness of his portrayal by the Spirit. The Son gives his life, death, and Resurrection to the Spirit, so that the Spirit can portray it through the people who lived through it all with him. His portrayal is such that it corresponds to the plan of the Father and expresses in the most vivid way the whole obedience of the Son and his conformity to the will of the Father. But the Spirit is not alone. He works together with those who love the Lord. The Son's gift to the Spirit becomes his gift to all Christendom through the apostles.

The Church can hold fast to what the Spirit has portrayed with a vitality in which the wind of the Spirit is perpetually blowing. The inspired character of Scripture is a confirmation of the Son's Ascension into heaven. At Pentecost he sends his Spirit to the apostles, but to all those of his own who exercise an apostolic ministry he gives the story of his life in an ever new way. He does not want to have his life at his own disposal. It was in the will of the Father that he lived his life; it was the Father's will that in his life he revealed; and it was according to the Father's will that he let himself be resurrected. So he does not want to be in charge of his life now, like someone who has had some experience and constantly talks about it. No, it is part of his perfect self-giving that he continues to be given in heaven, in the sense that he entrusts the story of his self-giving to the Spirit. It is entrusted to the Spirit, who henceforth does not work on his own, but with the cooperation of Christians. The Spirit has been received by them, with them he blows, and through them he wants to waft through the whole world. The Scriptures contain no retractions on the part of the Son. The Son does not say, "It was different from this, more could be said about it", or "No human being will ever know what I went through in the temptations", or "I could have told the whole story better myself", and so on. No, it is an essential part of the Spirit's role in the redemption of the world that this portrayal and exposition and inspiration are his work.

The great rhythm of heaven, the speaking and the keeping silent (mentioned earlier), blows through heaven. Ultimately, we should leave it to the Spirit to portray the life of the Lord in the way that the Spirit finds to be most in harmony with the will of the Father.

Almost nothing is said of the thirty years of the Son's contemplation. This is a sign of the Spirit's reserve. His conduct is in line with St. Ignatius' remark in the *Spiritual Exercises*: "The Scriptures presuppose that we have an intellect." In fact, especially for the most spiritual things, the Spirit depends on the Spirit in man, on the working of the Spirit in baptism and confirmation.

On the Night in the Second Week

Rest in heaven. Rest corresponds to the heavenly silence, which is day and action in relation to heavenly speech. This rest is in a special way at the disposal of all who keep watch and pray during the night. It proceeds from the triune God, but it involves in a special way the Blessed Mother. One might almost say that she enjoys more rest than is in accordance with her state, for the reason that she wants to make a gift of rest. She responds with rest to all restlessness. This goes beyond [St. Augustine's] "My heart is restless until. . .", because Mary gives rest beforehand to help us endure the unavoidable restlessness of the day and its questions and anxieties. The restlessness of the world is not taken away, but man is strengthened, so that more can be expected of him.

Then there are the many angels flying through the night and coming to earth with a thousand kinds of tasks. Mary is their Queen. They pay her homage by taking up her tasks, by being her messengers in this world. They work, educate, inspire, not by their own initiative, but as those who have been sent. I never knew until tonight just how much the angels are under obedience. I didn't realize that their mission and the carrying out of their mission and the account they give of it could be seen so clearly.

There is the possibility of sharing in the rest of the Mother by becoming more restless oneself. We should like to help her. We notice how her rest grows as we ourselves have more restlessness to bear. We cannot decide to do this by ourselves. We have to do it as a task with which we have been entrusted. There is a twofold restlessness: one that we take over, in order to take it away, from the restless man, but also another, which the Blessed Mother takes away. In the smallest of small things. As, for example, when someone needs rest in order to work and gets it and then has a hard time dealing with his own affairs.

Eucharist

We imagine heaven as a place existing in its own right and with various points of contact with the world. Certain actions of heaven would then be like flashes of lightning coming down to earth, striking it or not striking it. . . .

But the Eucharist proves to us that heaven really does have the capacity to hug the earth closely to itself, in a permanent contact, in an embrace. The Eucharist appears then as a state. As a state with the power to join heaven and earth together. The Eucharist embraces the whole life of the Son from the decision to become incarnate to the Last Judgment; it is not restricted to his thirty-three years of earthly life. It is already present *in nuce* in the Word of the prophets, because this Word was the Son, and in the meals that prefigure the bodily presence of the Lord in the sacrament. Through bodily presence he wants to communicate the Spirit of his love to men, a thoroughly heavenly love, which can be understood only in a heavenly way.

But we are human beings and are resurrected through the power of the Eucharist, and so what we understand of heaven is very much bound up with our humanity and cognitive powers. This does not make it less true. Nothing of what we grasp in faith of the eucharistic Lord is a lie. It is just that we are not in a position to put its various aspects into their mutual relationships. We cannot fathom the spatial and temporal aspects of the Eucharist, because space is infinite and time eternal, and it is only in the Lord that we have a sense of the eternal. The understanding of the eternal is very much the affair of the triune God, so we need not delve into it; we should be content with what is communicated to us of the mystery. The Lord gives us a truth, and we are responsible for its protection and must not overlay it with speculations about things that have not been disclosed to us. We understand only fragments of what is heavenly. Say, an artist had painted countless pictures throughout his life, and we had time to see three of them. We could not know to which periods they belonged, and still less could we reconstruct the whole body of his work.

The Passion

When we meditate on the Passion, the whole of heaven prepares itself, as it gazes on the Father, for receiving the suffering of the Son through the Father. The fact that the whole of heaven is looking at the Father is part of the Son's abandonment during the Passion. The Son knows—for example, in Gethsemane—that his obedience lives in the saints and angels, that they are gazing on the Father in his place, that they have taken over his vision of the Father. When he gives back his Spirit to the Father on the Cross, that same Spirit is received by all who gaze upon the Father, so that he can then be handed over to the Son. When the Spirit is handed over, the Son does not gather together the saints of the Father; they are already gathered to the Father, and it is in gathering that the handing over of the Spirit takes place. True, it is the Son who redeems these saints, as he redeems all men, but he wants them to experience the act of redemption through the Father. "This is a hard saying; who can hear it?" The Son makes a hard saying for himself out of the fact that he allows everyone to gaze upon the Father.

The Son suffers historically on earth, and opposite him stands the fullness of heaven. It accompanies him into the Passion, but it leaves him alone in it. There is nothing tragic about this. There is not just a heightening of the darkness; more profoundly, there is a heightening of the self-giving. The Son in his total darkness must not get any kind of comforting signal from heaven. The whole story of the Passion can be, so to speak, reconstructed from the viewpoint of heaven. The eyes of all turn more and more to the Father, to receive from him what he feels is good for us to be shown and given from the Passion of his Son.

The Resurrection

When the Son rises from the dead and ascends into heaven, he takes with him a body and thereby crowns the Father's creation. He is showing the Father that he is not only obedient unto death, but obedient unto Resurrection. His obedience has not only led him into the narrowing funnel of death but also widened into all the width of the Father and of heaven. And he comes with a body that comes from the Father's creation. He goes to heaven with a glorified body, and those who see him ascending realize how much at ease the Son is with his body, that he has made it his chosen body. He finds it so good that he not only enjoys it but gives it away eucharistically, hands it over for others to enjoy, and then, in a Eucharist for the Father, he brings about the resurrection of all flesh. He thus shows the Father that man, created by him, has a body that is worthy of eternity and the presence of God.

The eyes of heaven, which followed the Son on earth and into hell, are now, through him and his bodily Resurrection, turned again upward. Everyone had been looking down. After seeing in the Father the Cross of the Son, they had also beheld his descent into hell. But now the Son comes up to them in the body with the power to bring about the resurrection of all flesh. He has conquered the devil, sin, all that is vain and passing, has taken the chastisement on himself and extinguished it, and has given back the world to the Father. The redemption is not a mere leveling of the score but an overwhelming victory: the Son brings men into heaven as his brothers and children of God. Through the Resurrection the distance between heaven and earth is overcome.

The Assumption of our Lady into heaven has a deep connection with the Resurrection and Ascension of her Son. One of the qualities of the Mother's body that is taken up into heaven is also a quality of the Church. I sense the bodiliness of both the Lord and his Mother and the bodiliness of the Church, which connects both. I feel that, through her connection with the Lord and his Mother, the Bride-Church has permanent existence in her materiality, in her rock-ness, in her whole being. There is a mutuality of Bride and Bridegroom which in heaven can be felt sensibly. The visibility of the Church, comparable to a cathedral, has its counterpart in heaven, whereas her material quality is for this world of time; it will disappear, leaving only the "structure" of the *communio sanctorum*, and this will have an even more nuptial character. The relationship will be quite different from what it is now, just as the relationship of a father and mother to their children when small is quite different from what it is when they have grown up.

When the whole Church has become heavenly, because everything earthly has ascended into heaven, the relationship of heaven to earth will be objectless. But this redundancy makes room for new relationships. Love will be more free. Care will be different: it will no longer be anxious concern, but concern for, concern about. No relationship created by God leaves behind an empty space when it goes away; it is transformed into something higher.

(A. here says of herself: In heaven, when you see this correspondence of Christ and Mary, you can't see how you can go on living on earth. Everything corresponds so perfectly to what you desire—no, it goes far beyond that —to what you can desire. How can you still endure the pettiness of the world? It's obvious that the superabundance you receive in heaven can't be lived on earth. And yet I should bring the two into harmony. It's like having to put on a shoe that's much too big and one that's too small at the same time; it's very tedious. I can see that vision on earth and vision in heaven exist for each other; they're meant to be complementary, even now. In heaven you give yourself totally, but then the warning voice of the earthly, demanding its rights, is heard. It's a difficult business getting the balance in the center of yourself, because does the human person have a center? It's as if finitude and infinity, comprehensible and incomprehensible, were meeting in me [or someone else]. But the clearer the incomprehensible becomes, the more you have to grow into an obedience without face or form, an obedience whose demands are fulfilled in Christ and Mary, in the Trinity, in the whole structure of heaven. For the individual himself, they go beyond any earthly demand, beyond any ecclesiastical concern, beyond any divine demand on a man, and yet they are a mission in the mission, inexhaustible. The inappropriate element in it is predominant, and the appropriate, what can be comprehended, translated, appears, on the basis of the incomprehensible, simply petty. I understand: for the future there is only one thing to be done: to keep the appropriate open to the inappropriate, in a conflict that is unresolvable and yet without sadness.)

John and Peter

When God, the Father, the Son, and the Spirit, dwells in a heaven known only to them (because the world has not yet been created), love and order are one and the same. There seems to be no possibility of distinguishing them, because love is order and order is love. Each of the three Persons of the Trinity loves the others out of a divinely ordered love. They are distinguished from each other in a love that is order, and all that they are is ordered into love.

When God the Father, then, creates the world, he creates a world order out of love. He shows that there has to be order in the succession of his visibly ordered deeds. Even though those deeds come from infinity, they still have a sequence, through which an ordered world arises out of a disordered chaos. This order signifies a differentiation in love.

Finally man is created, and he is meant to have dominion over material things and animals. This dominion represents the vertical dimension in the order of creation. It is somewhat comparable to the order between Father and Son within the Godhead, in which each Person has his place, the order in which the Holy Spirit of Love is breathed forth. When the Woman eventually comes into Paradise, a horizontal joins the vertical; there is an order of "association". Before sin this association is totally unambiguous and unbroken and visible and a sign of God's love. Then sin comes along and brings disorder, a chaos that is not, as the first one was, purely neutral. But when the Son comes into the world, he brings with him the order of his world of love, and when he creates the Church as his Bride, he creates anew the order of love within her.

In heaven I saw how the triune God and the angels and saints and the whole heavenly Church do not simply approve of this relationship of order and love, of Peter and John, but actually love it and see in it the possibility of giving the Church the imprint of God. God's imprint is to be seen not only in theory but in practice, which ought, of course, to resemble the love of heaven: Peter steps forward, while John steps back and then steps forward again (Jn 20). This order is absolutely necessary for the earthly Church. If the boundless love of John were not subordinated to Peter, it would be unendurable for the earthly Church, which is made up of sinners. Is it not surprising that Peter, who three times denied the Lord, is the representative of order? Love in the newly created order is atonement for his denial, but it is also a sign that the sinner must be conscious of the fact that he is too weak to live without order and subordination. But if it is precisely to Peter that the superordination is entrusted, this is testimony to the confidence of Father and Son in the efficacy of redemption. There is nothing for which sinner can reproach sinner. Instead, sinner must show love to sinner, saint must show love to saint, the Church must show love to all believers in a form that in each case knows that love is greater than order but that God does not want a disordered love. Thus the symbol of order is the symbol of man's submission to love. And though Peter takes over from John by confessing that he "loves more" (Jn 21), he knows that he has to add the greater thing, love, to his lesser thing, office, that office must be lived out in love, so that it contains love within itself as, so to speak, the substance of its life. As in a communion.

It is strange, and yet in heaven it is proved to be true, that the saints and angels are very interested in Peter and in office. They want to love not merely at random, but by inserting their love into office. The heavenly Church keeps an eye on the structures of the earthly Church. She accompanies the feast days of the Church's year somewhat in the manner of an adult fitting in with the world of children.

Contemplation De Amore

The whole atmosphere of heaven is love. It is the first and last thing you see, because it runs through everything. But it never becomes a norm, because it is always over-flowing; it cannot be treated like something with fixed dimensions. There is no possibility of getting closer to it, or of moving away from it, or of considering it with a particular intention. We cannot grasp it; it grasps us. I don't know what it's like for those who are always in heaven, but for people invited to visit, it is a searing experience. You feel you're not a match for love. This is no inferiority complex; it's just that if you have double vision, you can see where love is lacking all over earth. You see it with new eyes, eyes that recognize the fact of the matter, not the state of individual people. Then there are moments when you really can dive into love. This is a delight, but it is a burning delight, like a yearning fulfilled. You don't even know that the object of your yearning is love; the yearning is too great for that. But everything you experience or would like to say comes from love and speaks its language. If you meet Mary on earth, I wouldn't say that the encounter can be captured in a conversation (it's just not possible), but somehow it can be taken up into a conversation. It can take that form or the form of a meditation or an idea or a piece of work. But if you meet Mary in heaven, or if you meet someone who is always in heaven, then what you are doing, what you are, is each time taken into something that is greater. You don't recognize yourself in it, but heaven.

On earth we might have a conversation and share our thoughts in order to reach an outcome that can be summed up in a concise sentence. What you say to me is the outcome of things you have thought or heard or read, and so on. In heaven, though, love is never the outcome of something. It runs through everything.

The strange thing is that for the person invited into heaven there is something provisional about all this. But the provisional is decked out in the definitive, the absolute. I know that what I have been given exists within and comes from absolute love, but in me there is a limit, which indicates the provisional nature of what is happening. And when on earth I run into a limitation, a lack of love in the apostles or in my fellow men, I know at the same time how different love is in heaven, and how much heavenly love has to flow into earthly, so that the lack can be remedied.

Love seems like a river that at any moment can provide you with what you desire. If you wanted to bathe, it would be just fine for that purpose. If you wanted to travel on it, say, on a boat, you could do exactly that. If you were thirsty and wanted to drink from it, its water would be drinkable. If you wanted to paddle in it, you could do so without getting out of your depth. It's as if the supreme law of this river is to be an answer for every- thing. At the same time, I don't know what the relationship is between the desire and its fulfillment. I do know, though, that you can ask the river questions (it's an open question whether these are inspired by the river of love) and that each of its answers is a fulfillment. It may be that, to begin with, you're a little frightened of the river, but then suddenly you notice that the streaming waters sweep you off to greater achievements, enable you to experience more things. To begin with, you may not want to lose the ground beneath your feet, and you practice swimming movements on the bank, but suddenly you long for something greater, for the greatest thing of all. This desire is a gift, and you find yourself in midstream, encountering the very waves for which you yearned. And then suddenly again it is all quite different, but you can't discern a pattern, an order, with human senses, because it is God's order, which is much greater than anything our sense of order can understand. The river can at the same time disappear and be ever present, be at once a raging torrent and a few drops on the bank. This river of love is in constant contact with the world. It seeks to refresh the world, to keep its resources unfailingly at the world's disposal. If it is turned down, there is no real disappointment in heaven, because it is then taken up into heaven. Of course, heaven would like the river of love to reach all men and bring them home. But if that doesn't succeed, the saints aren't sad, and when they intervene in person in the world's events and offer their services, this comes from a love that is inexhaustible and never disappointed. Disappointment does not penetrate heaven from earth. A limit is imposed—just as God's wrath was warded off by the redemption of the Son.

ABBREVIATIONS

AL   *Aus Meinem Leben*, 1968.

G   *Geheimnis der Jugend, Nachlaßbände* [Posthumous works], volume VII.

N   *Das Allerheiligenbuch* [The book of all saints].

T   *Erde und Himmel: Ein Tagebuch, Nachlaßbände,* volumes XIII–X.